The Baptized Body

Published by Canon Press
P.O. Box 8729, Moscow, ID 83843
800.488.2034 | www.canonpress.com

Peter J. Leithart, *The Baptized Body*.
Copyright © 2007 Peter J. Leithart.

Cover design by David Dalbey.
Interior design by Jared Miller.
Printed in the United States of America.

Library of Congress Cataloging-in-Publication Data

Leithart, Peter J.
 The Baptized body / by Peter J. Leithart.
   p. cm.
 ISBN-13: 978-1-59128-048-4 (pbk.)
 ISBN-10: 1-59128-048-6 (pbk.)
 1. Baptism. I. Title.

 BV811.3.L45 2007
 234'.161--dc22

                                    2007010661

09 10 11 12 13 14   10 9 8 7 6 5 4 3 2

The Baptized Body

PETER J. LEITHART

canonpress
Moscow, Idaho

Contents

Preface

In addition to being hurried and unpolished, *The Baptized Body* is a narrow and polemical little book. It is narrow because it focuses on a single question in the theology of baptism—the question of baptismal efficacy: What does baptism do to the baptized? That is an important question, but it's far from the only important question regarding baptism and, to my way of thinking, far from the most interesting question about baptism. I'd much rather be writing a book about the typology of baptism, or examining the social and political import of baptism, or even considering how post-Reformation changes in baptismal practice helped to forge modern civilization. Perhaps someday I can turn back to those subjects. As it happens, the question of baptismal efficacy is the most contentious question concerning this sacrament in the Reformed world today. Hence this book.

And so to the polemics. The polemical character of this book is somewhat oblique. I only rarely name people I'm disagreeing with, and I spend virtually no time evaluating and refuting their arguments. There is a reason for that: I don't want to condemn this book to a two-week shelf life. The question of baptismal efficacy is a perennial one in the church, and it will remain an important question when all the current controversies are a dim memory. When all the dust has settled, when advocates of "Federal Vision" or "Auburn Avenue" theology are either expelled from every major Reformed denomination or grudgingly permitted to stay, when goings-on in Moscow, Idaho, are a faint memory even for those who specialize in the arcana of American church history, I'd like this book to remain useful. It would please me if this book made some contribution to resolving today's disputes. I'm not expecting that to happen (truth be told, I'm expecting the opposite), but it would please me. It would please me far more if a reader with no knowledge of these disputes could happen upon this book in the dusty backroom of a used book shop long after I'm dead and find it edifying.

I've mentioned "Federal Vision" theology. I couldn't help but do that, since I wouldn't be writing this book if the Federal Vision had not become a controversial "movement" in the Reformed world. As much as I'd like to avoid mentioning it, now it's done, on the page, and no turning back. What can I say to that? What is the Federal Vision?

There is as much controversy about what the Federal Vision is and what its advocates teach as about the particular issues involved. That's partly due to diversity among the Federal Vision advocates themselves. It's also partly due to the fact that some associated with the Federal Vision are speaking what amounts to a different theological language from their counterparts. As a friend put it, Federal Vision theology sounds like speaking in tongues to some in the Reformed world. Finally, it's partly due to the fact that when mud is slung, few mud-slingers can rival Reformed mud-slingers.

Whatever the reasons, Federal Vision theology has been described as works-righteousness, covenant nomism, sacerdotalism, sacramentalism, Arminianism, Amyraldianism, Eutychianism, the road to Catholicism, Scotism, and many other things. According to some, the Federal Vision represents another gospel, and for some in the Reformed world the Federal Vision is so perverse that its advocates cannot be considered Christian brothers. It has confusingly been conflated with the New Perspective on Paul, and older controversies about the work of Norman Shepherd have been stirred in to add flavor. For some, the central problem with the Federal Vision is that it denies justification by faith, which no one has ever done; or election, which no one has ever done either. For others, the central problem with the Federal Vision is that it denies the imputation of the active obedience of Christ, a doctrine considered by some to be so central to the gospel that anyone who questions it almost ceases to be a Christian. Some say the Federal Vision teaches that all the baptized are savingly united to Christ, and so it leads to presumption; the same people, in the same breath, say the Federal Vision teaches that some in the church will fall away, and so undermines assurance. It teaches that we can trust in baptism; it teaches that we cannot. It teaches salvation by obedience; it teaches antinomian trust in external rituals. It teaches that we have assurance through baptism; it teaches that we have no assurance at all. Indeed, it is a strange and multi-headed beast, and it has awakened dragon-slayers and would-be dragon-slayers throughout the Reformed world.

What is at the heart of the Federal Vision? I cannot speak for all those wearing the FV logo, but in my view the Federal Vision is centrally about the issues I address in this book: Baptismal efficacy, to be sure, but more importantly and fundamentally, the nature of signs and rites, the character of the church as the body of Christ, the possibility of apostasy. At its heart, the Federal Vision is about ecclesiology, the doctrine of the church. The most important chapter in this little book is the third, "'The Body of Christ' Is the Body of Christ." As I see it, the Federal Vision's central affirmation is this: *Without qualification or hedging, the church is the body of Christ.* Everything the Federal Vision says about baptism, about soteriology, about apostasy flows from that affirmation.

This central affirmation may seem uncontroversial, and at one level it is: Every Christian says the church is the body of Christ. The nub of the debate is how that affirmation is developed and unpacked. On this issue, much that the Federal Vision says has roots in the Reformed tradition, and some associated with the Federal Vision are quite traditionally Reformed in their sacramental theology and ecclesiology. Others, such as myself, are more critical of some aspects of traditional Reformed theology and suggest revisions, some of which have radical and wide-ranging implications. Yet, I hope even at my most "radical," I have remained true to one of the most fundamental of Protestant commitments, namely, that

Scripture—not tradition, not even the Reformed tradition—is the final rule of faith and practice.

I like to say that the whole project is an effort to drag conservative Reformed churches, all kicking and screaming, into the twentieth century, the century of ecclesiology.[1] With this little book, unpolished and polemical, narrow and hurried, I hope to drag us all a few more inches.

---

1. That is not a lapse or a misprint. I know we've been in the twenty-first century for the better part of a decade. One has to start somewhere and temper ambition with realism.

1
Starting Before the Beginning

To understand baptism, we need to start not *at* the beginning—with the various passages that deal with baptism, the mode and subjects of baptism, and so on—but *before* the beginning. We need to begin with the unexamined and often false assumptions about God, man, the world, the church, salvation, rituals, and signs that shape and sometimes control our theology of baptism.

Paul writes that the Roman Christians have all been united to Christ in His death and resurrection by baptism (Rom. 6:1–7). Paul is so sure the Roman Christians already know this and agree with him that he makes this point as a question: "Do you not know that all of us who have been baptized into Christ Jesus have been baptized into his death?" (v. 3). He expected the Romans to answer, "Oh, yes, of course we know that." Yet, many cannot take Paul at his word. According to them, "baptism" doesn't refer to the "sign" of water but to the "thing" that the water symbolizes. Paul isn't talking about the baptismal rite itself. He isn't telling the Romans they were dead and risen with Christ by *baptism*, but by that to which baptism points.

Which raises three basic questions: First, if he didn't mean baptism, why did he say baptism? Second, how do these commentators *know* Paul wasn't referring to baptism? Third, what assumptions about the world drive this interpretation? Why would anyone doubt that Paul is talking about water?

One can answer the first question by observing that the word "baptism" can have a variety of meanings, so, the question is always what that word means in a particular context. I'll address that problem at length in chapter 2, where I'll argue that "baptized" in Romans 6 refers to the water-rite of Christian baptism.

Another answer to the first question goes something like this: "There is a 'sacramental union' between sign and thing. They are distinct but not separable, and therefore the writers of Scripture sometimes refer to the 'sign' when they are talking about the 'thing.'" By this argument, however, any passage about sacraments can be turned into a passage that is *not* about sacraments. Does Paul say that the loaf is a "communion" with the body of Christ? Well, he doesn't mean the actual physical loaf, but the "thing" to which the loaf points. We can read 1 Corinthians 10:16–17 and remain safely Zwinglian. Does Peter say that "baptism now saves you"? Well, he isn't referring to water, but to that which the washing points. "Baptism now saves you" is a colorful way of saying "Christ now saves you." "Baptism now saves you" means "'Baptism' now saves you."

This is hopeless. By this procedure, we can neutralize any passage about the sacraments. In the end, we will have no sacramental theology and perhaps no sacraments.

The answer to the second question—how can anyone *know* Paul is not talking about water baptism?—is closely bound up with the first. Readers know that Paul was not referring to water baptism in Romans 6 because water can't do the things Paul says "baptism" does here. It's self-evident that water cannot join us to the death, burial, and resurrection of Jesus.

Why then does Paul use the word "baptism"? Because the biblical writers sometimes refer to the "sign" when they mean . . . You get the point. That is precisely the argument in John Murray's *Christian Baptism*, still very much a standard treatment of the subject in Reformed circles. Though Murray doesn't go so far as to say that "there is no water in Romans 6," he does say "it is not the rite of baptism that is in the foreground" because the "thing" of union with Christ is in the foreground. With a wave of his hands and a few irrelevant quotations from other Pauline letters, Murray concludes that "reference to the rite may have receded almost to the point of disappearance." This is not a cogent argument because it is not an argument at all. It is assertion.

The answer to the third question is found in, with, and under these assertions. A pile of rotting assumptions lies buried in Murray's analysis that needs to be respectfully exhumed and given decent but decisive burial. For instance: One reason for denying that "baptism" in Romans 6 refers to the Christian rite of initiation is a fear of attributing too much power to water. In his recent systematic theology, Robert Reymond, in the tradition of Murray, argues that, despite speaking of sacraments as "effectual means of salvation," the Westminster Confession and Catechisms make it clear that "there is nothing in the sacraments *per se* that saves." Armed with this assumption, a commentator is almost forced to conclude that Paul is not talking about water. If he were, then he would be attributing power to the sacrament itself. Hence:

1. *Paul says the baptized are united to Christ in His death and burial, so that they may be raised.*
2. *We know that water-baptism doesn't have this kind of power.*
3. *Therefore, Paul cannot be talking about the water-rite.*

Anyone who thinks Paul is attributing power to baptism can be neatly dismissed with a single old Princetonian sneer: "Sacerdotalist!"

Seas of ink have been poured out in debating whether there is any efficacy in the sacraments "in themselves." The whole debate is worthless, because both sides begin from the false assumptions that 1) there is such a thing as a "sacrament in itself" and that 2) some things (though not sacraments) do have "efficacy in themselves." Consider: Baptismal water is a sign authorized by Christ for His church. Validly administered, it is *never* simply water, but the authorized entry rite into the community of disciples (Mt. 28:18–20). We cannot, we dare not, think that this water is "mere water," any more than we can think of the American flag as "just a piece of cloth." Water is not a "thing in itself."

Besides, whatever could it mean for sacraments to operate "by themselves"? We can only believe this possible if we believe that the world has some degree of autonomy, that the creation has some power or will or force of its own. Reformed people above all should know this is folly. Is it possible for water to exist at all apart from the continuing work of the eternal Word of the Father, who holds all things together, including hydrogen and oxygen atoms? Not if we take Paul seriously. Does the water that washes what remains of my hair in the shower work "by itself"? God forbid! Does the bread I eat on Monday provide life "by itself"? Nothing at all, other than the Triune God Himself, has efficacy "in itself."

I'm not disputing the Reformed answer. The fact that the question has been raised and taken seriously demonstrates the need for a root-and-branch reform of our baptismal theology. Before we can progress in providing answers about baptism, we have to repent of our questions.

Baptism and the Real Me

Some of our bad questions arise from a faulty view of man and of personal identity, a faulty view that is largely a product of modern individualism.

Baptism is about personal identity. It answers the question, "Who am I?" As I've noted, Paul expects the Romans to know that "all of us who have been baptized into Christ Jesus have been baptized into His death" and reminds them that "if we have been united with Him in the likeness of His death, certainly we shall be also in the likeness of His resurrection" (Rom. 6:3,5). Because they are joined to Christ by baptism, the Roman Christians are to "consider [them]selves to be dead to sin, but alive to God in Christ Jesus" (Rom. 6:11). To use the modern jargon, Paul teaches that a Christian's "self-image" is grounded in and shaped by the fact of his baptism.

But is this really true? Is the "self-image" that comes from baptism accurate, or is Paul playing a game of "let's pretend?"

Sprinkling a few drops of water, especially on an infant, can't change who he really is. It might affect him in some "external" and "legal" ways, but it cannot touch his core identity. To be blunt, if Abdul is a rank unregenerate unbeliever a moment before baptism, he is still a rank unregenerate unbeliever a moment after baptism. Abdul is still Abdul, even if he's wet. To suggest otherwise is to transform the sacrament into superstition.

That seems reasonable, and yet Paul says, "All of us who have been baptized into Christ Jesus have been baptized into His death" (Rom. 6:3). How can we make sense of Paul?

For starters, the ("Protestant") notion that baptism does not affect the "real me" and the apparently opposite ("Catholic") notion that baptism supernaturally infuses a habit of grace that transforms the soul both assume the same view of personal identity. Protestants deny that water sprinkled on my body changes the "real me" be-cause the "real me" is a soul tightly and hermetically sealed within my body. If baptism is going to affect me in any fundamental way, it has to be something more than water applied to my body. It has to be infused with magical or supernatural power to penetrate past my skin and touch my heart.

Catholics also deny that an external rite can change who I am, and for the same reason as Protestants, namely, because the "real me" is locked up inside my body. For Catholics, if baptism is going to affect me in any fundamental way, it has to be something more than water applied to my body. It has to be magical, supernatural.

Catholics, of course, believe that baptism injects supernatural power, Protestants don't. But this difference pales in comparison to the more basic agreement between the two, and this fundamental agreement explains why debates between the Protestant and Catholic are so frustratingly inconclusive: How can you begin a debate, much less win it, when your opponent already more than halfway agrees with you? Behind both views of baptism is the notion that the "real me," what makes me uniquely me, is some internal ghostly me that remains unaffected by what happens outside and is unchanged by what happens to my body. Neither the Protestant nor Catholic considers a third option, the possibility that baptism, precisely as an *external* and *physical* ritual, might actually affect who I am. Both the Protestant and Catholic, in short, seek to locate some eternal, unchangeable, autonomous "me" deep within. Ultimately, this is idolatrous. It is an effort to find some divine me inside the human me. Christians aren't supposed to believe in any such thing.

We can make the point by looking at what the Bible says about the soul and the "inner man." Let's assume for the sake of argument that "soul" in the Bible means "the real, inner, essential me." Even if we adopt this questionable definition, it is clear that the "real, essential me" is affected by the world and by external events. According to Scripture, souls, and not just bodies, hunger and thirst (Ps. 107:9), and hungry and thirsty souls are refreshed when they receive physical food and drink (1 Sam. 30:12). Spanking a child drives foolishness from his heart (Prov. 22:15), and the Torah of Yahweh, which comes as ink on a page or sound waves on the air, restores the soul (Ps. 19:7). When it seems that God is absent and enemies have been unleashed to destroy him, David's soul "pants" for God to come and deliver (Ps. 42:1; cf. vv. 9–10). David would have difficulty singing "It is well with my soul," for when disaster strikes, it is definitely *not* well with his soul.

The fact that the Bible often describes the "inner" man by reference to bodily organs (heart, kidneys, liver) is another hint that Scripture does not sharply distinguish inner spiritual realities from outer physical realities. Even the "inner" man is conceived physically, not as a disembodied, ghostly self. There is always more to a human being than appears on the surface, but being human is always "being in the world" because it is always "being a body." What makes me uniquely me includes what happens to my body.

The point is not that there is no distinction between "inner" and "outer." There is. The tabernacle and temple, which are among other things architectural representations of man, have an "inner" and an "outer" court, and Paul speaks of "inner" and "outer" man (Rom. 7:22; 2 Cor. 4:16; Eph. 3:16). But there is no impermeable membrane between my inner life and my outer life. My inner thoughts and desires come to outer expression, but by the same token what happens to me on the outside affects my inner man. Inner and outer are two dimensions of one united human life.

Given this biblical anthropology, we can see how external events, like baptism, might affect the person as a whole. A non-priest becomes a priest through the rite of ordination, a single man becomes a husband through a wedding ceremony, a private citizen gains public authority by inauguration. These new identities *are* new identities: The ordained *is* a priest, the man a husband, the citizen a President. We would not say there is some non-priest lurking under the skin, or the President is only "externally" President. Why should we say there is some "unbaptized" self inside the baptized?

Whatever else we must say about a baptized person (and we will say much more), we can say with utter confidence that he is *baptized*, that a minister has poured water on his body in the name of the Triune God, and that this is an irreversible event in his "being in the world." He emerges from the waters of baptism, and that fact alone means he is a new person. He has received a new name, a new identity, a new past, and he is called to a new future. Abdul is no longer simply Abdul, and he is not simply wet Abdul. Abdul is *baptized* Abdul. That means the "real Abdul" has been changed.

Baptism and the Social Contract

Some of our bad questions are reinforced by bad political theory. What does baptism have to do with politics? you ask. Ahh, that is precisely the problem. That's one of the questions we need to repent of.

During the Middle Ages, baptism was considered not only a rite of initiation into the church, but an entry into a general citizenship. Priests kept baptismal records not only in service to the church, but as a civil registry. A study by Italian scholars Elena Brambilla and Joaquim Carvalho notes that

> Baptism was first and foremost among the sacraments defining, symbiotically, religious together with civil membership: on the one hand it defined compulsory religious affiliation to the only true Church and the only true Catholic faith; on the other hand it determined membership of all individuals, or of the faithful, to that lower, basic level of civil rights or "civil" citizenship which

included all men, rich and poor, women, infants, serfs and slaves, excluded from active or political citizenship.

The novel and revolutionary idea that baptism was a purely religious rite, without any civil implications, took off only in the sixteenth century, among Anabaptists. Anabaptists baptized only professing adults, but the scope of their revolution was much broader. They aimed to uncouple religious and political affairs and undermine the foundational structures of Christendom.

We are all, more or less, Anabaptists now. Few if any advocate a return to a baptismal reckoning of civil rights. Anabaptists certainly made some gains. By undermining Christendom, they also undermined a lot of what must have been hypocritical conformism. Yet, there is, I think, a case to be made for the older practice. Whatever their political allegiances, Christians who baptize babies implicitly confess that religion and society are inseparable.[2]

For the moment, my concern is not with baptismal citizenship but with another dimension of the connection of baptism with politics. Specifically, I submit that our views of baptism have been deformed by the individualistic politics of the modern age.

According to the great American Catholic thinker John Courtney Murray, John Locke's political theory envisions human beings as hard atoms of human nature. They bump into each other and bounce off each other, but like billiard balls they retain their shape no matter how much of a beating they take from others. Insofar as it is Lockean, modern liberal politics assumes this atomistic view of human nature, which is incompatible with any strong view of baptism. Can a little sprinkle of water change the condition, color, or character of a billiard ball? Of course not.

Social contract theory assumes this vision of human existence. According to the social contract myth, human beings are isolated Egos. Each of us has a will of our own, and each is free to make choices on our own. We are "I's" first of all, though we may, for various selfish reasons, combine with other "I's" into political society. To put it grammatically, though each "I" might address someone else

2. For more discussion along these lines, see the Appendix.

as a "you" and might even combine with others to form a "we," the "I" remains the first person not only in our grammar charts but in social fact.

As the German-American sociologist Eugen Rosenstock-Huessy frequently protested, however, everything we know about actual human life leads in the opposite direction. We don't begin life as isolated "I's." Infants have little consciousness of their own bodies. They can't recognize themselves in the mirror. They have no consciousness of being "I's," but they are aware quite early of certain significant others. A baby's world is not centered in her Ego. It centers on others who speak, coo, sing, hum, kiss, nuzzle, smile. These and dozens of other forms of communication are all, grammatically, in the "second person," saying "you" to the child.

Our grammatical texts lie to us. As Rosenstock-Huessy says, the grammatical second person is the existential and social first person. Were it not for the inane mythologies of social contract theory and liberal politics, this would be more than obvious. Once it's pointed out, it *is* obvious. Our children only speak in the first person after they have been addressed in the second person; our children develop a consciousness of self after and through their consciousness of others; infants develop a sense of personal identity because we talk to them using names they didn't choose.

What is perhaps not so obvious is the import of this discussion for baptism. This will become clearer when we ask . . .

Do Baptists Talk to Their Babies?[3]

Protestants have always emphasized that salvation comes through faith, yet most Protestants have baptized babies. How can these two things hold together? Luther and Calvin held together their insistence on faith with infant baptism by claiming that infants can believe. Baptists see this as the Achilles' heel of the paedobaptist position, an example of absurd lengths to which paedobaptists are willing to go in defending an untenable practice.

---

3. The substance of this section was first published as "Do Baptists Talk to Their Babies?" in *Rite Reasons* 47 (September 1996), available at: www.biblicalhorizons.com/rite-reasons/no-47-do-baptists-talk-to-their-babies

Is infant faith absurd? "Faith" is the human response of trust toward God, a response of allegiance, in a personal relationship, and this has large consequences for our understanding of infant faith. The question of infant faith is not: "Are infants capable of receiving this jolt of divine power?" The question is: "Can infants respond to other persons? Do infants have personal relations?" And the answer to this question is obviously yes. Infants quickly (even *in utero*) learn to respond to mother's voice; infants quickly manifest "trust" of their parents; infants quickly distinguish strangers from members of the family. If infants can trust and distrust human persons, why can't they trust in God? Behind the denial of infant faith is, apparently, an assumption that God is less available to an infant than other humans. But this is entirely wrong; for no human being is nearer than God. And it is wrong because God's presence is mediated through His people. When parents say to their newborn, "Jesus loves you and will care for you," they are speaking God's promises.

Parents, moreover, establish relationships with their infants through symbols. We talk to our infants, and we show our love through gestures such as hugs and kisses. If there is nothing irrational or absurd about humans establishing a personal relationship with infants through symbols, there is nothing irrational about God doing the same. As we establish loving and trusting relations with our infants through symbols, so God speaks to infants and establishes a relation with them through the "visible word" of baptism. Thus, the question "Should we baptize babies?" is of a piece with the question "Should we talk to babies?" Paedobaptism is neither more nor less odd and miraculous than talking to a newborn. In fact, that is just what paedobaptism is: God speaking in water to a newborn child.

If the child cannot understand what a parent is saying, is it rational for the parent to speak to him or her? Baptist parents as well as others speak to their infants and do not expect the child to understand or to verbally respond for many months. They see nothing irrational in this. They speak to their children, that is, they employ symbols, not because they think the infant understands all that is being said or because they expect an immediate response. They speak to their child so the child will learn to understand and talk back. So too, we baptize infants and consistently remind them of their baptism and its implications so they will come to understanding and mature faith. We name them so they will grow up to respond to that name; we speak to them so they will begin to speak back; we name them in baptism so they will begin to live in and out of baptism.

The sociologically consistent Baptist should, it seems to me, allow children to name themselves. Otherwise, they are inevitably "imposing" an identity on their little boys and girls. Karl Barth, who loudly protested the "violence" of imposing a Christian identity on a child through infant baptism, would undoubtedly be pleased. In fact, Baptists don't do this, but they do impose a language on their children. They do, in spite of themselves, often treat their children as Christians, teaching them to sing "Jesus loves me" and to pray the Lord's Prayer. And if they do all this, what reason remains for resisting the imposition of the covenant sign?

Having cleared this political ground, we are in a better position to understand . . .

Why Sacraments Are Not Signs

I admit it: Sacraments are signs. Though the New Testament never speaks of baptism or the Lord's Supper as "signs," Old Covenant "sacraments" are described in these terms. Following Genesis 17:11, Paul writes of "the sign of circumcision," which was "a seal of the righteousness" that Abraham possessed by faith before he was circumcised (Rom. 4:11). The blood of the Passover lamb was a "sign" (Exod. 12:13), and the Passover meal together with the Feast of Unleavened Bread was permanently "a sign to you on your hand" and "a reminder on your forehead" (Exod. 13:9).

In the face of this evidence, I stand by the title of this section, which is not meant merely as a provocation. Though sacraments are called signs in Scripture, we need to explore what "sign" means, because many Christians, both today and in the past, have understood "sign" in an unbiblical fashion. Popular conceptions of "sign" and "symbol" are erroneous in a number of respects, but in this section I discuss only one error, namely, the tendency to treat signs rationalistically, as nothing more than means of communicating ideas from one mind to another mind. In this sense, the title is completely accurate—sacraments are not signs. Or, more precisely, if sacraments are signs, they are also much more.

For many, signs function cognitively or didactically, enabling us to pass on ideas to other people and to remember or consider concepts, ideas, and things. Applied to the sacraments, this view of signs implies that baptism informs us about our state of original sin, our need for cleansing, the coming of the Holy Spirit, and the sprinkling of our hearts with the blood of Jesus. Baptism exists mainly to *teach* us something. (Obviously, this view raises virtually unanswerable questions about infant baptism.) The Lord's Supper, similarly, reminds us of the death of Jesus and teaches us that He is our life.

Sacramental theology has employed this idea of signs for a long time. Augustine defined a sign as "a thing which of itself makes something come to mind, besides the impression that it presents to the senses" (*On Christian Teaching*, 2.1), and Augustine's definition was the basis for sacramental theology throughout the Middle Ages and into the Reformation. The seventeenth-century Reformed theologian Francis Turretin explained that sacramental signs work in such a way that "the thing promised is so represented to our minds that it is caused also to be truly communicated."

Though not wrong as far as he goes, Augustine does not go nearly far enough, and the application of his definition of sign to sacraments has been the source of much confusion. To be sure, the Bible does speak of signs that "call things to mind and memory." The rainbow was set in the sky as a reminder of Yahweh's covenant (Gen. 9:12–13, 17), and Aaron's budding rod was kept as a memorial of Aaron's status and God's judgment against rebels (Num. 17:10). Frequently, however, "signs" in Scripture are given not to be looked at or contemplated but to be *done*. The Sabbath is a sign (Ezek. 20:12, 20), and this sign would certainly teach the Israelites something about Yahweh's salvation of Israel. Yet, Israel would not have been faithful if they had done nothing more than contemplate or think about the Sabbath; they had to keep and sanctify the Sabbath. Applied to the Sabbath, a sign is not something that brings another thing to mind, but a significant practice, an *enacted* sign.

Many uses of "sign" in Scripture, moreover, refer to God's actions, particularly His works of power against Egypt (Deut. 4:34; 6:22; 7:19; 11:3; 26:3; 29:3; 34:11; Ps. 78:43) or Jesus' miracles among the Jews (Jn. 2:18, 23; 4:48, 54; 6:26; 9:16). Augustine's definition of "sign" doesn't easily fit these passages. God did indeed communicate with Pharaoh through frogs and lice and pestilence. Far more than that, however, God *did* something to Pharaoh, and by doing so demanded Pharaoh do something in response. God made Himself known to Pharaoh, but not with a chart or a theology text. He made Himself known by confronting Pharaoh in power, by getting in Pharaoh's face with a series of overwhelming, awesome signs.

Another problem with Augustine's definition of sign is brought out explicitly in the quotation from Turretin. As Keith Mathison has put it in his fine study of Calvin's Eucharistic doctrine, *Given For You*, "For Turretin, the connection between the signs and the things signified is a connection that occurs in our minds." Turretin claims there is a "spiritual presence" in sacraments but only in the sense that "the things signified are present by their signs, whose nature is to make another thing come into the mind and so place the thing before the senses or mind." Mathison shows in detail that this was not Calvin's teaching about the relation of signs and things or about "spiritual presence," but Turretin's conclusion seems almost inevitable if we start from Augustine's definition of signs. If a sign is given "to bring something else to mind," then the marriage between the sign and reality takes place within our heads. Augustine's definition robs sacraments of much of any objective, real-world efficacy. On these assumptions, sacraments do nothing but provoke pious thoughts.

From a biblical perspective, to call sacraments "signs" brings out several dimensions: a) as signs, sacraments do communicate; they mean something, bring something to mind, and are intended to teach; b) but as signs sacraments are also *actions* performed at God's command by the church; and c) as signs sacraments are mighty acts of God for the redemption of His people and the world. If "sign" means all these things, then baptism is most definitely a sign.

If "sign" is not the best term to describe sacraments, perhaps we can call them "means of grace." Perhaps, but I don't think this gets us where we want to go. I have to show now . . .

Why Sacraments Are Not Means of Grace

Theology ought to be precise. As one Puritan said, we serve a precise God, and we ought to imitate him. Precision is not a problem. The problem is pseudo-precision—confusion masquerading as clarity. This is a common malaise, and perhaps most especially in sacramental theology. Instead of actually explaining how sacraments do what sacraments do, many sacramental theologies put on a show of explanation that amounts to little more than thick fog that wraps the unwary and prevents them from seeing they have entered a cul-de-sac.

One example of this problem is the use of the phrase "means of grace" as a description of sacraments. The language of "means" has an ecumenical pedigree that appears frequently in Reformed theology and confessions. According to the Westminster Larger Catechism, God enables us to "escape the wrath and curse of God due to us by reason of the transgression of the law" by making "diligent use of the outward means whereby Christ communicates to us the benefits of his mediation." Among these means "whereby Christ communicates to his church the benefits of his mediation" are "word, sacraments, and prayer; all of which are made effectual to the elect for their salvation" (questions 153–154).

To the extent that the idea of "means of grace" emphasizes that believers receive real benefit from baptism and the Supper, it is a helpful corrective to feeble theologies that are widespread in the modern church. And, to the extent that the phrase is used to emphasize that *God* bestows life through water, bread, and wine, it is a useful reminder not to make idols of the elements. In several respects, however, describing sacraments as "means of grace" can be misleading and adds unnecessary complication.

We can get a sense of the problem when we attempt to apply "means" language to other areas of life. Is the sentence "food is a means of nourishment" any more precise than "food nourishes"? Is the claim that "water is a means for washing" better than "water washes"? Is sex a "means of making love" or is it "making love"? In each case, sticking "means" into the sentence gives the impression of insight and precision, but without much payoff. More seriously, sticking "means" into the sentence gives the impression that "nourishment," "washing," and "love" exist apart from means and have to be "channeled" through means, as if washing or nourishment or love were some very, very fine kind of substance that has to find a thicker embodiment in the "means" of water or food. In fact, nourishment only exists by our eating food, washing only with water, and love in bodily expressions. "Means" explains nothing.

Talking about the sacraments as "means" tends to mechanize them, turning the sacraments into machines that deliver grace. Sometimes, the mechanistic imagery is explicit. Thomas Aquinas, for example, tried to explain how sacraments worked by referring to Aristotle's view of causation. God is the "principal cause" of the grace of the sacraments, which means that God acts through sacraments. So far, so good. But then Thomas goes on to compare the causative power of sacramental elements to a hammer in the hand of a carpenter (i.e., God). Is it useful to describe sacramental causation by comparison with physical causes? Do signs "cause" in the same way as tools?

More fundamentally, mechanistic metaphors obscure the fact that sacraments are moments of personal encounter with the living God, "trysting places" between God and His people, as Luther liked to say. The Reformed tradition has defined the sacraments as "signs and seals of the covenant of grace," thereby highlighting the covenantal and interpersonal character of the sacramental event. Unfortunately, the "personalism" of this covenantal theology has often been undercut by the notion of sacraments as "means."

At its best, covenant personalism is an expression and expansion of fundamental Trinitarian theology. Though its radical implications have not always been recognized, Trinitarian Christianity is fundamentally hostile to all forms of impersonalism. The debates concerning the Trinity in the early church elevated "personhood" and "personality" to an ontological status. As John Zizioulas puts it, for the early fathers, being *is* communion. God didn't first exist as a monad or an unrelated substance and then proliferate into three persons; that would make unified being more original than diverse communion. Nor did God first exist as three separate individuals who later entered into a divine social contract for their mutual protection and benefit. God has always been three Persons in perfect loving communion; God has always been the One God; He exists as the One God as three Persons. Communion is the eternal, necessary form of God's existence.

This marks a revolution in thought. Greeks could not conceive of a *personal* absolute being because they couldn't conceive of an absolute being who was in relation to other beings. Relation means relativity. For the Greek mind, as soon as the absolute being is in a necessary relation with another being, the absolute being ceases to be absolute, and is "relative" to another. As soon as the absolute being is personal, it ceases to be absolute.

Trinitarian Christianity confessed the unthinkable, a Personal Absolute, an Absolute Person, an Absolute Communion, a Communitarian Absolute. Trinitarian Christianity confessed the unthinkable, that the Absolute God was necessary related to and relative to other persons who were also, impossibly, Absolute God.

Think of the Athanasian arguments for the eternity of the Son: If the Son is not eternal, then the Father is not eternally Father. If the Son came into being at some (timeless) moment in eternity, then the Father became Father at that same (timeless) moment. If the Father is eternally, necessarily, unchangeably Father, he must eternally, necessarily, and unchangeably have a Son. At the same time, Athanasius notices that the Father's Fatherhood is entirely dependent on the fact that He has a Son. The Father's character as Father is *relative* to the Son; He is Father in relation to the Son. As Augustine later points out, Father, Son, and Spirit do not name three "substances," nor are these the names of three "accidents" in God. Rather, Father, Son, and Spirit are spoken of God (in Edmund Hill's accurate but clumsy phrase) "relationship-wise."

In this way, Trinitarian Christianity cleared out the clutter of mediating powers and emanations and beings that the Hellenistic mind had used to fill the space between God and His creation. God is through-and-through personal and relational, both in Himself and in His relationship to the creation. He speaks the world into existence by the Person of the Word, and He forms the ages by the same Word (Heb. 1:1–3). He speaks to clouds, and they bring rain and snow. He shouts and a forest topples. He calls out, and the wild donkeys give birth.

Particularly as God deals with human persons, He acts as Person, as Persons. He shares a meal with Abraham outside his tents, announces the birth of Samson to Manoah's wife, inspires the prophets to speak His word to the wayward kings of a wayward Israel. In the last days, the Son comes in flesh to speak and listen, to feast and mourn, to weep over Jerusalem and at the tomb of Lazarus, to suffer death and rise again. Every good thing we receive is a gift of God, a gift that expresses the eternal, unutterable kindness of our Creator.

The phrase "means of grace" obscures the personal dimension of the sacraments when it is allied with a depersonalized misunderstanding of grace. In Scripture, "grace" means essentially God's personal favor. Noah "found favor in the eyes of the Lord" (Gen. 6:8), and Abraham's prayers were premised on the "favor" he had found in the sight of Yahweh (Gen. 18:3; 19:19). A sinner receives grace when God overlooks and cleanses his sins and receives him into fellowship. God's favor is expressed in various gifts or "graces." A king who receives a servant into his favor gives him provisions of various sorts; Hrothgar expresses his favor to his warriors with gifts or rings or gold. Yahweh is Israel's "ring-giver." In Scripture, the Lord's gifts include promises, land, seed, rescue from enemies, victory in battle, commandments, fellowship with God, the Spirit's presence, rituals, enlistment in God's people and God's army. These graces to Israel are all gifts of grace, expressions of God's personal favor toward His people.

Shortly after the apostolic period, this concrete and personal understanding of grace and graces began to slip away. Theologians began to treat grace as a kind of "created thing," "force," or "energy" communicated through various means, including the sacraments. Grace is not God's favor, but a kind of fluid that can be poured into human hearts through the funnels of the sacraments. Ultimately, this model rests on a mistaken doctrine of God. For Trinitarian Christianity, as I've emphasized, there is no impersonal force in God, nor is there any "energy" that mediates between God and creation. The "force" that acts on us, whether in sacraments or ordinary food or washing, is God Himself. God Himself acts on the creation in His Word and Spirit.

The model of the sacramental operation should not involve four terms—God, grace, sacraments (as "means" or "channels" of grace), church; but only three—God (who is favorably disposed to us), sacraments, and the church. In the sacraments there is a personal encounter with the Triune God through the particular agency of the Spirit. The Jews marveled at the change that came about in the disciples, and noted that they had been with Jesus (Acts 4:13), and the same is true for us who have not encountered Jesus in the flesh—we are transformed not by impersonal energy flowing from God, but by a personal encounter, in word and water, in bread and wine, with the Lord who has become a life-giving Spirit (1 Cor. 15:45; 2 Cor. 3:17–18). We are transformed when God shows His favor through granting favors, when God shows His grace through bestowing graces.

I suggest the following refinement of the confessional language: Instead of saying sacraments are *means* by which Christ's benefits are communicated to us, we should simply say the sacraments are among the benefits that Christ has graciously given to us. Sacraments are not means of grace, but themselves graces, gifts of a gracious God. They are benefits that manifest and communicate the God who favors us.

Why Sacraments Are Not Symbols

If "means of grace" doesn't work as a definition, maybe sacraments are symbols, then. Not really, at least not in the sense Lady Macbeth discussed symbols.

Scottish nobles were arriving for the feast, but their host was, yet again, "rapt." Ever the attentive (and pestering) wife and hostess, Lady Macbeth urged her husband to greet his guests:

> My royal lord,
> You do not give the cheer. The feast is sold
> That is not often vouch'd, while 'tis a-making,
> 'Tis given with welcome. To feed were best at home;
> From thence the sauce to meat is ceremony;
> Meeting were bare without it.

Alas. For all Lady Macbeth's attentions, the feast is a disaster, for reasons wholly outside of her control—visions of bloody ghosts, Macbeth's outbreak of insanity, interruptions by hired thugs. The stuff of Martha Stewart's nightmares.

For Lady Macbeth and many Christians too, ceremonies and symbols are more or less unnecessary adornments or enhancements of real life. The key assumptions in this view are a) that natural or literal reality can be isolated from its enhancements, b) that natural or literal reality is non-symbolic, and c) that "real [i.e., non-symbolic] life" is the foundation on which we set up pretty symbols. These assumptions are false.

Sharp distinctions between sauce and meat, between normal/natural and ceremonial, or between "literal" and "symbolic" dissolve on inspection. With regard to language, there is no clear line between literal and symbolic. In an important sense, all language is "symbolic" because it employs visual symbols or sounds that mean something other than themselves. Even if we put that point to the side, it is still evident language exists on a spectrum from less metaphorical to more metaphorical language. There is no clear boundary line.

Most readers, for instance, will have understood the previous paragraph as primarily literal, yet I have employed several figures in the course of my argument: No one is really drawing lines between literal and symbolic words, and those non-lines are not literally "clear." Distinctions are not literally "sharp," I am not "making" "points" (as if this were an exercise in pin-production), and no reader is actually being asked to put my "points" to the "side." The moment we speak, we use language that is always already symbolic.

Lady Macbeth was most completely wrong to believe that it is possible to have a "meeting" (even a naked one) without ceremony or symbol. Language and other symbolic acts create, renew, or maintain personal relations so that there can be no meeting without symbol. Coming into a party full of strangers, you spy a familiar face in a small but lively circle near the *hors d'oeuvres*. As soon as you enter the circle, you begin to deploy symbols, and are deployed to. You use language: "Hello!" "Bon jour!" "Hola!" "Guten Tag!" You exchange greeting gestures—a handshake, a kiss, a hug, a significant exchange of looks, a secret fraternity rite. Should your friend introduce you to the other members of the group, you speak, shake hands, smile. Without these symbolic actions, these meaningful uses of the body, no personal relationship would be established.

Or: A young man is desperately in love with a young woman. He thinks about her day and night, dreams about her, hears her voice in his mind's ear, imagines what it would be like to hold her hand, to kiss her, to take long moonlit walks with her. This might go on for years and years without becoming an actual romance. If he is going to move from internal feelings of infatuation and an imaginary romance to the risky but more pleasurable relationship with a real woman, he must "go public." And he does this through symbols. He speaks or writes to her, employing linguistic signs; he sends flowers, which he intends as an erotic symbol rather than an encouragement to horticulture. She will respond, if she responds, with symbols—words or significant actions—which will imply something on the spectrum between invitation and scorn.

In these examples, symbols do not dress up and enhance a relationship that already exists; we are not back to Lady Macbeth and her saucy meats. On the contrary, relationships do not exist at all apart from the symbolic and ceremonial exchanges. We cannot say, except as a joke, "I know him/her well, we're great friends, but we've never spoken or written or exchanged greetings."

Relationships do not exist "behind" the symbolic exchanges, as if the "real relationship" were a hidden "spiritual" reality of which the symbols are only visible or audible "expressions." Our pining lover might find comfort in Lombard's definition: The signs he uses are, he might hope, "visible signs of an invisible relationship." An invisible romance is better than none! But no; Lombard offers false comfort. Without signs there is no romance, not even an invisible one.

What does this all have to do with liturgy and sacraments? If sacraments are signs and symbols in the sense suggested here, then they are (with the Word and through the Spirit) the matrix of personal communion with the Triune God. The symbolism involved in sacraments is the symbolism of action, less like the symbolism of a painting or a metaphor than the symbolism of a handshake or a wave or a kiss. They are symbols by and through and in which personal, covenantal relationships are forged and maintained. God Himself is invisible, and there are also invisible aspects to our relationship with God. Of course, God is not locked out from a comatose human being who cannot sense or respond to any external signs or words. In all normal circumstances, however, the invisible features of our relation with God occur within the framework of visible signs, rites, and seals that constitute the covenant. Sacraments are not "signs of an invisible relationship with Christ," as if a relationship with Christ might occur without them. Rather, the intricate fabric of exchanged language, gesture, symbol, and action *is* our personal relationship with God. This is the fabric of "favors" that expresses God's personal "favor." These are the graces that exhibit God's grace, the gifts that connect us again and again with the God who gives.

Sacraments Are Rituals

So. If sacraments are not means of grace, or signs, or symbols, what are they? In some respects, they are in a category all their own. In fact, it is not entirely helpful to talk about baptism and the Supper under the single category of "sacraments." Still, if I have to pick a general category that covers both, I would pick "ritual." I have several reasons.

First, many of the traditional descriptions of sacraments fail because they obscure the fact that sacraments are actions. By contrast, "rite" and "ritual" immediately imply action. Scripture highlights this by the terminology and descriptions of sacraments, particularly in the Old Testament. Exodus 12:26 uses the word "service" with reference to Passover (Exod. 12:26), and the Hebrew word, *abodah*, frequently means "labor" or "work." Further, the sacrificial sacraments of Leviticus consist of a carefully prescribed set of actions. Contrary to the impression given by the popular dictum, "add the word to the element and it becomes a sacrament," baptism is not merely the "element" of water plus the word. For a baptism to take place, water must be used in a particular way. The Supper is not merely bread + wine + the Word, but bread-and-wine-eaten-and-drunk-by-the-Church, plus the Word.

Further, by defining sacraments as "rites," we move away from a narrow focus on the physical elements or on the visibility of the elements. To speak of sacraments as rites emphasizes that they are performed by a community and are embedded in the life of that community. From this angle, baptism may be seen as a "rite of entry" that expresses the character of the church—that it is a community where racial, economic, and sexual divisions are dissolved (1 Cor. 12:12–13; Gal. 3:27–29). When we all partake of one loaf, the church is publicly and ritually expressing that she is one body in Christ, her many members working together for the edification of the whole. The ritual becomes a standard against which we measure the quality of our life together.

Understanding sacraments as rites also helps us to understand the efficacy of sacraments. Certain Puritans (and Lady Macbeth) to the contrary, rites and ceremonies are not mere window-dressing added to an occasion that could take place without ritual and ceremony. Rites accomplish what they signify. As an "initiation" rite, baptism is analogous to other rites of entry into organizations or groups. To reiterate what was said above: When one is admitted to the bar, he has to go through certain formalities, and at the end of the ritual process he becomes an attorney. Going through a wedding ceremony creates a marriage and transforms a single man into a husband and a single woman into a wife. Ordination turns the candidate into a minister, a swearing-in ceremony makes a person a judge, and an inauguration—presto!—makes a President. Rites do not recognize a status that already exists; they place a person in a new status.

Scripture shows the reality of status-changing rites. A child circumcised on the eighth day becomes a child of the covenant, and an unclean person who undergoes the prescribed washings is made clean (Lev. 15). In the ordination of priests, to take another example, the priest offers a bull for the sin offering (Lev. 8:14–17). Bulls are used for purifications only for priests or the whole congregation (Lev. 4:3, 13–14), so the fact that Aaron uses a bull in the ordination rite is fitting. Other elements of the purification in the ordination rite, however, are not consistent with the purification of priests. In Leviticus 4, the purification of a priest requires the blood to be sprinkled before the veil of the sanctuary and on the horns of the altar of incense (Lev. 4:5–7), but this is not what happens in the ordination rite. Instead, the blood is put on the horns of the altar of burnt offering and the rest is poured at the base of the altar. Thus, the purification rite is and is not like the purification for priests, and the reason is clearly that at the beginning of the rite Aaron was not yet a priest. During the rite, Aaron's sin offering was performed in one fashion; the next day, it would have to be performed in another fashion. His status changed because he went through the rite of filling.

Importantly, through this rite Aaron's status changed *before God*. When two people marry, their status changes from "single" to "married," and what happens through the rite of covenant-making is said to be something "joined together" by God. A week before the wedding, sex between the engaged couple is fornication and a sin; on the wedding night it is no longer a sin. To become a priest was not merely to enter a new social status or a new position in a religious organization. Once ordained, Aaron was allowed to approach the tabernacle without being killed, because Yahweh had accepted him as a temple servant. Once ordained, he received a privileged nearness to God that was denied to others.

To call the sacraments "rites," therefore, is to emphasize that they actually accomplish and do things, changing status, altering personal identity, and expressing God's favor. God recognizes the baptized person as a baptized person and a member of the body of Christ. God regards a church that celebrates the Supper as a church that has celebrated the Supper. Conceiving sacraments as rites underscores a strong view of the efficacy of sacraments, but there's no magic of mumbo-jumbo here. As rites, sacraments are effective in the same way that words are effective. There's magic in the sacraments in the same sense that there's magic in the words "I baptize you in the Name of the Father, Son, and Spirit" or "I now pronounce you man and wife."

God, Time, and Change

One of the key background issues in sacramental theology has to do with God's relationship to time. No one believes God is bound by time. No one involved in these debates is an "open theist" who believes God is incapable of knowing the future. Everyone confesses that God is unchanging in His being, wisdom, purposes, plans. He has planned everything He is going to do in history, and everything He's going to do with us. He is Alpha and Omega and knows, and determines, every end and every beginning. Every last detail of history is under God's control, and that includes the not-so-insignificant detail of who lives and who dies eternally. God is the Playwright, and before He drew back the curtain, He had not only formulated the Dramatis Personae, but had written out everyone's actions and destiny to the end of time.

For some, however, God's transcendence of time effectively cancels out any real interaction or involvement that God might have with creatures in time. Because God has determined and knows that some person will be reprobate, He cannot really, sincerely favor that reprobate in time. Because God has scripted history and fixed the course of events, God never really reacts to our actions. When the Bible says "God changed His mind," it is mere anthropomorphism.

This is not a satisfying answer. The Bible says God changed His mind, and the Bible is true (Exod. 32:14; Jer. 26:19; Amos 7:3, 6). The Bible also says God does not change His mind, and that is also true (1 Sam. 15:29). We should try to affirm both equally well, and not allow one biblical truth to cancel another. Any time our theology makes it difficult or impossible to say what Scripture says, our theology must be mistaken.

From the first chapter of the Bible, we find that God is both creating time (which means He's not controlled by it) and working *within* time. He sets up the sequence of dark and light that constitutes the time-period called the "day." Once He finishes establishing that pattern, however, He works within it. He does particular things on particular days, apparently ceasing from work during the darkness of night and definitely ceasing from work on the Sabbath that crowns the creation week. Yahweh doesn't have to rest, and in some sense, as He is "pure act," He works continuously (Jn. 5:17). Yet, the Bible reveals that God operates within the constraints of time as well.

We can go further. The Creator not only follows the temporal pattern established on the first day, but He also responds to what happens on each day following. Each day of the creation week, He speaks something new into existence. He speaks, and waters divide to reveal dry land. He speaks, and plant-yielding trees appear. He speaks, and the waters swarm with fish. He's the one working each day through His Word, yet at the end of each day, He passes judgment on what has come to pass. On each day but the second, He looks at what He Himself has done and says, "This is good." At the end of the week, the commendation is stronger: "This is very good" (Gen. 1:31). In other words, God not only initiates everything each day, and throughout the whole creation week, but also responds to what He has done. He commands and then reports on the accomplishment of His commands. Because He is Alpha and Omega, He both issues imperatives and passes an indicative judgment on what He has done.

That initial revelation is borne out throughout the Bible. God does all things according to the counsel of His own will (Eph. 1:11), and yet God also responds to, reacts to, and passes judgment on things that He Himself has performed. He responds to prayers with showers of blessings. He responds to rebellion with flaming wrath. He mourns over the city and the people that refuse to receive Him. God, the changeless God, is a responsive God.

Here again we see one of the radical implications of Trinitarian theology. If God is eternally One, there is no other to respond to, until God creates an other. That makes his responsiveness a secondary acquisition, as if he is trying out a new gait. A unitarian god can become responsive only at the cost of his changelessness. Since God is Triune, however, He is eternally responsive. Father, Son, and Spirit live in an eternal communion of love, gift, delight, and joy, giving to and receiving from one another in an eternal round. The Triune God does not become responsive when He makes a world; but because He's Triune He is capable of responding to the world. The rhythms of the life of Father, Son, and Spirit constitute the uncreated archetype of created time. Creation moves in time because God is Triune, and God is capable of working within time because He is Triune.[4]

God is changeless, but we must define changelessness the way the Bible does and in a way consistent with our Trinitarian convictions. We must be careful not to fill the word "changeless"

---

4. More speculatively, but I think plausibly: God is capable of both initiating and passing judgment because He is Triune. The Father creates through the Son and Spirit, and when the Father judges that all is "good," He is not patting Himself on the back but commending the work of the other Persons. Similarly, the Father judges the Son favorably in the incarnation.

with whatever content we think is appropriate. For instance, one might argue: God is changeless; any action is a change; therefore, God doesn't really act. When the Bible says He acts, it's speaking "anthropomorphically." But that's not the way the Bible defines "changelessness." Obviously God does act, and all the time; He works from the beginning until now, Jesus says. We can't conclude from God's changelessness that God is motionless.

In short, we should affirm both sides of this apparent contradiction between God's changelessness and His responsiveness. It is not a real contradiction. Even if they seem contradictory to us, for God they are perfectly compatible. But we can go further than this. There is a great mystery here, but the best thing to say is this: The biblical statement "God changed His mind" is true not *in spite of* the fact that He has planned and works everything, but *because* He works everything. God's plan, His will, His script, determines what is real in the creation, and God decreed the whole sequence of threatening-and-changing-His-mind. That must be real not *in spite of* being planned by God but precisely *because* it is planned by God.

The Westminster Confession wisely makes a similar point when it emphasizes that God's decree does not cancel the reality and efficacy of secondary causes but actually "establishes them" (3.1). I cause a table to be built. That doesn't make the saw and the hammer and the nails useless or irrelevant. Rather, the hammer and the saw and the nails and all come into their own only *because* I use them, because I'm the primary cause. The saw and hammer and nails don't get themselves organized to build tables. Without me, they aren't causes of anything. So also, when God uses the creation to accomplish things, He *makes* them causes. They would not be causes without Him as the primary cause. The creation doesn't organize itself to accomplish things. A created cause is a created cause only because it is used by God, who is the first cause. When God responds to prayer, for example, He really is responding to prayer. Prayer becomes a means for effecting the world because God uses our prayers to accomplish His purposes, not in spite of God's preordination of our prayers.

In short, God has planned everything, but part of what He's planned is a change in His relationship with us. This is not only explicit in various passages of Scripture, where it is said that God changed His mind, but it is evident from the very nature of the gospel. What can we say about a man who is a rogue apostate, living in flagrant disobedience to God, preying on every attractive woman he meets, backbiting his business associates and cheating his business competition? Are we justified in saying that he is the object of God's anger and wrath? Certainly. What if he converts? Has God's attitude toward him changed? Certainly. He has moved from wrath to grace; before God regarded him in Adam, but now He regards him in Christ. God had not shown favor; then He does show favor. That's what conversion means.

Conclusion

There are no doubt other false assumptions at work in sacramental theology that need to be exposed and corrected. We have, however, cleared enough ground to move ahead from our place "before the beginning." We're ready to begin.

2

"Baptism" is Baptism

Peter tells the crowd at Pentecost that they should "repent, and let each of you be baptized in the name of Jesus Christ for the forgiveness of your sins; and you shall receive the gift of the Holy Spirit" (Acts 2:38). Paul says virtually the same later in Acts, recounting his own conversion: Ananias said to him, "And now why do you delay? Arise, and be baptized, and wash away your sins, calling on His name" (22:16). The link between baptism and forgiveness of sins is not merely sequential. According to Peter, the repentant are to be baptized unto (Greek, *eis*) the forgiveness of sins, and the gift of the Spirit follows on that baptismal cleansing (cf. Ezek. 36:25–27). Ananias's words to Paul imply, as G. R. Beasley-Murray says, "his sins will be washed away in his baptism accompanied by prayer."[5]

Similarly, in Romans 6, Paul appeals to baptism as evidence that the Romans have been joined to Jesus' death and resurrection: "do you not know that all of us who have been baptized into Christ Jesus have been baptized into His death?" (v. 3). Verse 4 is even stronger, emphasizing the "instrumental" character of baptism: "we have been buried with Him *through* (Greek, *dia*) baptism into death," and this burial-through-baptism is done "in order that

---

5. A number of times in Acts, the gift of the Spirit is more directly associated with the apostles laying on hands (8:14–17; 19:1–7). Important as these passages are, they shouldn't be allowed to rob Peter's statement at Pentecost or Ananias's promise to Paul of their force. Besides, the notion that the Spirit is communicated by the hands is no easier to accept than the idea that the Spirit is communicated by water.

as Christ was raised from the dead . . . so we too might walk in newness of life." We die and are buried in baptism so that we can participate in new life in Christ.

First Corinthians 6:11 also describes the efficacy of baptism in striking terms. Having reminded the Corinthians of their lives prior to conversion, Paul says they have now been changed: "but you were washed, but you were sanctified, but you were justified in the name of the Lord Jesus Christ, and in the Spirit of God" (1 Cor. 6:11). "Washing" might refer to a "spiritual" or metaphorical cleansing, but there are good reasons to think this a baptism text. The only other use of the verb "wash" in the New Testament is Acts 22:16, which records Ananias's words about Paul's baptism. Further, the washing (along with sanctification and justification) is done "in the name of the Lord Jesus Christ," language that echoes baptismal formulas in Acts. A reference to washing "in the Spirit of our God" also brings up baptismal associations, especially in light of Paul's later statement about baptism in 1 Corinthians 12:13: "by one Spirit we were all baptized into one body." If 1 Corinthians 6:11 is a baptismal reference, it is a very striking one, because it links the washing of baptism with justification and sanctification (note the string of parallel "but you were's"). First Corinthians 12:13 is further evidence of Paul's strong view of baptismal efficacy, indicating that through the Spirit we are baptized into Christ's body.

Peter crowns this trend with the statement that "baptism now saves you" (1 Pet. 3:21). The qualification Peter introduces ("not the removal of dirt from the flesh, but an appeal to God for a good conscience") does not, as often thought, diminish the efficacy he attributes to baptism. It is not as if Peter says "baptism now saves you" and then adds, as a slight nuance, "but baptism doesn't really save you." On the contrary, the clause strengthens Peter's point about baptismal efficacy. This qualification makes no sense if Peter is merely contrasting baptism to a daily bath: Would anyone be tempted to believe baptism was a bath to remove dirt? If not, why does Peter make the point? As is clear from Hebrews, the contrast of "flesh" and "conscience" is one way of stating the contrast of Old and New Covenants (cf. Heb. 9:13–14; 10:22). And this is what Peter is talking about: Baptism, Peter says, does not remove fleshly defilement, as did the cleansing rites of the Old Covenant (cf. Lev. 15; Heb. 9). Rather, Christian baptism cleanses so that the baptized has "an appeal to God for a good conscience." The New Covenant washing has a power *greater* than the power of the Old Covenant sacraments. Christian baptism penetrates beyond flesh and its defilements to cleanse the conscience.[6]

Many Reformed folk are hesitant to use this biblical language, except in somewhat hushed tones. This is a trend of long-standing in the Reformed tradition, although the Westminster Shorter Catechism (#91) asks, "How do the sacraments become effectual means of salvation?" clearly implying that in some way the sacraments *do* become such. Along similar lines, Calvin said in a sermon on Acts 1 that "We are not so raw as not to know that the sacraments, inasmuch as they are helps of faith, also offer us righteousness in Christ. Nay, as we are perfectly agreed that the sacraments are to be ranked in the same place as the Word, so while the Gospel is called the power of God unto salvation to every one that believeth, we hesitate not to transfer the same title to the sacraments."

Of course, pointing out that the New Testament speaks strongly of the effect of "baptism" is not to explain what these passages mean. How are we to understand this efficacy? How can we say what the New Testament says without apology or hesitation, while also avoiding the very real and dangerous errors the church has fallen into throughout the centuries? Do we not diminish the role of faith if we speak of baptism as the rite by which we are united to Christ, as the washing by which we are justified and sanctified, as the event by which we are "saved"? How can we both affirm what the Bible affirms about baptism, without hesitation,

---

6. This interpretation is supported by an investigation of the word Peter uses for "dirt," *hrupos*. The verb form of this word, "to be filthy," is used in Revelation 22:11 to describe those who are excluded from the New Jerusalem. Filth in this context doesn't refer to dirt *per se* but to ceremonial and moral defilement. In Job 14:4 and Isaiah 4:4, two places where the Septuagint uses the word *hrupos*, the word also has the connotation of "defilement."

embarrassment, or bad conscience, while also avoiding the errors that have plagued the church for centuries? How can we affirm a strong view of baptism without implying that all the baptized are saved and without implying that baptismal water has become a magic potion?

"Baptism" is Baptism

I propose to answer those questions in terms of three axioms:

1. *"Baptism" is baptism. When the New Testament writers use the word "baptism," they normally mean the water rite of entry into the church.*
2. *The "body of Christ" is the body of Christ. When the New Testament writers call the church the "body of Christ," they mean the visible or historical church is the body of Christ.*
3. *Apostasy happens.*

Though numbers 1 and 2 may seem truisms or even tautologies, they are not, or at least they are not considered such by many Christians. They must be argued for.

Let's tackle the first axiom: "baptism" means baptism. This claim is questioned on at least two grounds. First, many believe it is impossible for water to do what the New Testament says baptism does. But this is, as I argued in chapter 1, often little more than an assumption brought to the text rather than a conclusion derived from it. It is equivalent to saying John's teaching that "The Word became flesh" doesn't mean "God became man" because we already know it is impossible for God to become man.

We do, of course, need to remember that when the word "baptism" refers to the water ritual, the writer is talking about baptism and not merely water. The word "baptism" in this sense is not even equivalent to the action of pouring water or dunking in water. We cannot reduce a wink to a blink, or a wave of the hand to a nervous twitch of the arm, or an execution by lethal injection to a murder. A wink is not a variation on a blink; it is simply a different action. A Nazi salute is a different act from brushing away an irritating dragonfly. Hanging is not necessarily a murder, though in both cases a person ends up dead. These actions are different because of the intentions and authorization of the actors. So also, baptism involves a particular use of water, a use authorized and commanded by Jesus Christ, and baptism is always done in connection with the Word. Therefore, the question is never "Can *water* do this?" but always "Can *baptism* do this?"

Second, some have pointed out that the Greek words for "baptize" and "baptism" (the nouns *baptisma* and *baptismos* and the verb *baptizo*) have a range of meanings in Greek texts and even in the New Testament itself. By itself, the word does not necessarily mean "water initiation." In the most elaborate study of the uses of *baptizo* in Greek literature, James W. Dale explains that in its original usage the word referred to physical immersion in a fluid. Yet, this was far from its only meaning. As Dale puts it, "Whatever is capable of thoroughly changing the character, state, or condition of any object, is capable of baptizing that object; and by such change of character, state, or condition, does, in fact, baptize it." Given the variety of its meanings, "the simple word baptize gives no authority to introduce water into any baptism." Yet, even Dale makes it clear that the word is commonly used for immersion in water or for various water rites. Josephus writes of ships "baptized" in the Adriatic (*Life*, section 3), and of Herod's plot to "baptize" Aristobulus in a pool until he drowns (*Antiquities*, 15.3). And the New Testament itself shows that Jewish rites of purification could be described as "baptisms" (Heb. 9:9–10).

Given this diversity, however, we have to look at context when examining the New Testament's use of this word group. Within the New Testament, some passages that use "baptism" clearly do not refer to a water rite. Jesus describes His death as a "baptism" (Mk. 10:38–9; Lk. 12:50) and the gift of the Spirit at Pentecost is also a "baptism" (Mt. 3:11; Mk. 1:8; Lk. 3:16; Jn. 1:33; Acts 1:5). In both cases, Dale would argue, the word refers to an event that exerts an overwhelming influence so great as to change the condition of the person who experiences the baptism. Baptism in these passages refers, Dale argues, not so much to the process involved as the condition that results.

Can we ever decide when the New Testament writers use baptism to refer to the water initiation of the church and when they use it in another sense? Perhaps all of the uses of the word "baptize" refer not to the rite of Christian baptism but to some overwhelming experience or event that effects a change in a person.

Context is king. In many passages, there is no doubt that "baptize" and "baptism" refer to a water ritual: either John's baptism (Mt. 3:7; Mk. 11:30; Lk. 7:29; Acts 1:22; 10:37; 18:25) or Christian baptism (Mt. 28:18–20; Mk. 16:16; Acts 2:38, 41; 8:12). In other passages, some form of the word is used in a context where *water* typology is clearly in view. When Paul speaks of a "baptism" in the "sea" during the Exodus (1 Cor. 10:2), he is thinking of the sea as the medium in which Israel was baptized. Similarly, Peter draws a typological connection between the flood and baptism (1 Pet. 3:18–22). It is hard to imagine that Paul and Peter would use the words "baptize" or "baptism" in these contexts without intending readers to think of the watery crossing, the flood, of their own water baptism.

Even without bringing other passages into play, these two passages suffice to show that the New Testament teaches a strong view of the effect and power of water baptism. Peter speaks of water baptism as a saving event, even as Noah and his family were brought safely through the water of the flood. Likewise, Paul claims that passing through the water baptism of the Exodus united Israel with her covenant head ("into Moses"), and we know from Exodus 14 that this event delivered Israel from Pharaoh and Egyptian power. In an important sense, we don't need to prove that other passages that use the word "baptism" refer to the water rite. We have plenty to go on in these two passages.

As a work of supererogation, however, we will examine those other passages. Can we tell whether Paul, Peter, and the rest are referring to the ritual of water baptism? I think we can.

Dead and Buried in Baptism

There is a range of opinion in Reformed circles about the meaning of "baptism" in Romans 6. On the one side, it does not appear to have entered Calvin's head to question whether Paul is talking about water baptism. In his commentary on Romans 6, he presents no argument for this interpretation but simply assumes it. He does contend that Paul uses the word "baptism" to refer to the "effect of baptism," since "it is beyond any question, that we put on Christ in baptism, and that we are baptized for this end—that we may be one with him." Throughout this sentence "baptism" means water baptism. He adds, "this power is not apparent in all the baptized," since some do not respond in faith. Paul emphasizes rather the "real character of baptism when rightly received." In short, "as long as the institution of the Lord and the faith of the godly unite together" we must speak as Paul speaks about baptism, "for we never have naked and empty symbols, except when our ingratitude and wickedness hinder the working of divine beneficence." John Murray to the contrary, Calvin does not think the rite recedes to the background here. For Calvin, baptism combined with faith brings union with Christ. Water baptism "rightly received" does what Paul says it does.

Likewise in the *Institutes* 4.15.12, Calvin cites Romans 6 to support his contention that "all those who don Christ's righteousness are at the same time regenerated by the Spirit, and . . . we have a pledge of this regeneration in baptism." Note that Calvin does not claim baptism effects regeneration (which, in any case, he often uses in a different sense than later Reformed theology), but he does believe Romans 6 refers to water baptism as the visible symbol pledging regeneration to those who have faith. It should be noted that Calvin's comments show that deciding whether or not Romans 6 is talking about water baptism does not by itself determine how baptism is related to union with Christ's death and resurrection. Calvin interprets water baptism as a "pledge" of new life rather than an instrument for delivering that new life.

The comments of the late James Montgomery Boice represent another interpretation. In his commentary on Romans, Boice,

following James Dale, warns that we should not too quickly interpret "baptism" in Romans 6 as a reference to water baptism. He
notes that the Greek word *baptizo* can refer to a radical and profound change, whatever the means of that change. He notes that
Josephus speaks, for instance, of crowds flooding Jerusalem and
"baptizing" the city, and when *baptizo* is used of a drunken person
("baptized" with wine) or dying cloth (cloth "baptized" in dye), the
emphasis is on the change that occurs rather than on the fluid used.
In Romans 6, Boice says, the main idea is "that we have been taken
out of one state and put into another" and that we are now "identified with him in (or baptized into) his death, burial, and resurrection." Water baptism *signifies* this transition but does not *effect* it.
In Romans 6 Paul is talking about the thing water baptism signifies
rather than about water baptism itself.

While Paul is teaching that the Romans have been "taken out
of one state and put into another," he is equally concerned that the
Romans *know* they have been taken out of one state and put into
another. The chapter begins with Paul addressing an antinomian
objection to the gospel: If, as Paul has announced, grace abounds
where sin increases, then should we sin to increase our dose of
grace? Paul responds by reminding the Romans that they have been
transferred from Adam to Christ; but, in addition, he points to an
event that made this transition apparent and, according to Paul's
instrumental language, *effected* this transition. That *event* and not
just its effects are crucial to Paul's exhortations.

We must also ask, if "baptize" here does not refer to the rite of
water baptism, what does it refer to? Boice's answer appears to be
that it refers to a conversion experience, the moment in a person's
life when they leave the Adamic realm for the realm of Christ. But
that answer presents a serious pastoral problem. What if one has
no conversion experience, or at least no memory of one? I myself
grew up in a Christian home, was baptized as an infant, and have
been a Christian for as long as I can remember. What would Paul
tell me? Of what radically transforming event would Paul remind
me? On what grounds would Paul tell me I have been turned from
the mastery of sin to the dominion of righteousness? When was I

buried with Christ so that I might live with Him? Paul's argument demands that the event he refers to is fixed, clear, public, datable.

It also demands something that is common to all Roman believers. He's talking about a universal Christian event or experience. Paul is explicit about this: *"all* of us have been baptized" (6:3). If this is talking about an overwhelming personal experience, it's hard to imagine what that could be. Even within the New Testament, we find a variety of experiences. Some become Christians in the blinding light of Jesus on the Damascus Road, while others slip almost imperceptibly from being eunuch God-fearers to being disciples of Jesus (Acts 8:26–40). Church history only enriches this variety. Some are made disciples by a rushing mighty wind, others by a gentle breeze and a strange warming of the heart. One might say that "all of us" experience this, but what strikes us is the variety.

So, the question in Romans 6 is: If Paul is not referring to the water rite of initiation, what is the alternative? Whatever it is, it must fulfill two conditions: It must be capable of being described as a "baptism," and it must be universal among Christians. The simplest answer is that Paul calls it "baptism" because it is.

N. T. Wright interestingly suggests that the sub-narrative underlying Romans 5–8 follows the story of Israel's deliverance from Egypt, from their enslavement to Pharaoh to their entry to the promised land. Romans 5:12–21 describes the reign of death (Pharaoh) which has been overthrown by Christ (the new Moses). In chapter 7, the emphasis is on the effects of the law, which only provokes sin from the fleshly people who receive it. In Romans 8, however, there is a promise of entry into a new creation, a land flowing with milk and honey, so long as we follow the cloudy pillar of the Spirit through the wilderness. Within this sequence, chapter 6 corresponds to the Exodus itself, Israel's deliverance from the mastery of sin and death and her enslavement to Yahweh. Fittingly, this transition is described as a "baptism," matching the water-crossing of Israel through the Red Sea. In short, though Romans 6 does not mention water, it is based on the same typology as 1 Corinthians 10.

Baptism into One Body

First Corinthians 12:13 is commonly seen as a reference to the experience of baptism by the Spirit rather than water baptism. No wonder. The text explicitly states that the Spirit is the agent (or the medium) by (or in; Greek *en*) which we are baptized: "by [or, in] one Spirit we were all baptized into one body." Craig Blomberg points out that there are seven uses of the phrase "baptize with/in the Spirit" in the New Testament (in addition to 1 Corinthians 12, he notes Matthew 3:11; Mark 1:8; Luke 3:16; John 1:33; and Acts 1:5; 11:16). These passages all contrast water baptism with the baptism of the Spirit. In Paul's usage, Blomberg says, the phrase refers to "an initiation experience that immerses a person into the realm of the Spirit." This Spirit-baptism "must not be confused with water-baptism."

Calvin is guilty of just this "confusion," however:

> Paul *of course* [emphasis added] is speaking about the baptism of believers, which is efficacious through the grace of the Spirit. For to many people baptism is merely a formality, a symbol without any effect; but believers actually do receive the reality with the sacrament.

Thus, "as far as God is concerned, it always holds true that baptism is an ingrafting into the body of Christ, because everything that God shows forth to us in baptism, he is prepared to carry out, so long as we, on our part, are capable of it." Paul has in view the "essence of baptism," which is "to incorporate us into the body of Christ," and this is the essence of baptism, Calvin argues, whether or not everyone who receives the sacrament is actually joined to Christ. Paul's point in mentioning the Spirit is simply to emphasize that "this is not effected by the outward symbol." It is rather the "work of the Holy Spirit."

So, who's confused? Calvin or Blomberg? Does "baptism" in 1 Corinthians 12 mean water baptism? There are good reasons to think so, and to accept Calvin's "of course."

First, baptism is mentioned several times in 1 Corinthians prior to chapter 12, and those uses are linked in various ways with

12:13. In 1:13–17, there is no doubt Paul is speaking of the rite of baptism since he speaks of an action that some human being, Paul or someone else, performed. In the first chapter, Paul points to water baptism as a sign of the unity of the Corinthians in Christ, and this provides an important link with 12:13, where he teaches that baptism forms one body that is not divided by ethno-religious or social boundaries. Paul also mentions baptism in his typological interpretation of the Exodus in 1 Corinthians 10:2, where he speaks of baptism "in the cloud and in the sea." As argued above, the reference to a baptismal experience in *water* makes it clear that he is thinking about water baptism, and the connections between 10:2 and 12:13 are tantalizing:

> Baptized into Moses in the cloud and in the sea (10:2)
> Baptized into one body [of Christ] in/by the Spirit (12:13)

Further, the last clause of 12:13 echoes 10:4:

> *All* **drank** the same *spiritual* drink (10:4)
> *All* made to **drink** of one *Spirit* (12:13)

The latter deliberately reaches back to the clearly sacramental references at the beginning of chapter 10. If Paul describes baptism in chapter 12 in terms similar to his description of water baptism in chapter 10, it's likely he's talking about water baptism in the latter passage as well.

Second, 1 Corinthians 12:13 more distantly echoes the baptismal passage at the end of Galatians 3: "all of you who were baptized into Christ have clothed yourselves with Christ. There is neither Jew nor Greek, there is neither slave nor free man, there is neither male nor female; for you are all one in Christ Jesus" (3:27–28). First Corinthians 12:13 also refers to baptism, unity, and the dissolution of boundaries between Jews and Greeks, slaves and free men. Below, I will examine Galatians 3. At this point, the argument is simply this: If Galatians 3:27–28 is about water baptism, there is good reason to believe the same about 1 Corinthians 12:13.

Third, what about those passages that use "baptism in the Spirit" with reference to something Jesus would do, in contrast to the water baptism of John? Particularly in Acts 1:5, this phrase refers to the outpouring of the Spirit at Pentecost, and I believe that's what the phrase "baptism with the Spirit" means throughout the New Testament. At that same event, however, Peter announces that anyone who wants to share in the baptism of the Spirit that occurs at Pentecost must "repent, and let each of you be baptized in the name of Jesus Christ for the forgiveness of your sins; and you shall receive the gift of the Holy Spirit" (Acts 2:38). In other words, the rite of baptism incorporates the baptized into the company of the disciples of Jesus, which is the body of Christ, where they share His Spirit.

Finally, the immediate context and argument of 12:13 makes a reference to water baptism likely. Verse 13 is arranged in a rather obvious chiasm:

A. By one Spirit
   B. We were all baptized into one body
      C. Whether Jews or Greeks
      C'. Whether slaves or free
   B'. And we were all made to drink
A'. Of one Spirit.

From this arrangement, it's clear that "all baptized" is parallel to, or perhaps equivalent to, "all made to drink." The two phrases have often been taken as references to the two sacraments. Calvin tentatively states his opinion that the latter phrase refers to the Supper "because he mentions drink, for I have no doubt that he intended an allusion to the analogy of the sign." Paul thus was pointing to the fact that "we share in the cup" so that "we may all drink the same spiritual drink." In the Supper, "we drink the life-giving blood of Christ, so that we may have life in common with Him; and that really happens when He dwells in us by His Spirit."[7] Plus,

---

7. John Calvin, *Commentary on I Corinthians.*

"drink of one Spirit" is linked to "drank spiritual drink" in chapter 10. If "drinking of the Spirit" does refer to the Supper, it is likely that "baptized with the Spirit" refers to the other sacrament.

The clearest evidence that Paul is talking about water baptism, however, is that all of 1 Corinthians 12 is about the visible church. Each member of the body has a "manifestation of the Spirit for the common good" (v. 7), the common good of the visible, historical community of the church. No member of the body can lord it over others, since all are necessary to the proper functioning of the body (vv. 14–21). This body is distinct from other social bodies in that the "least honorable" members receive more abundant honor (vv. 22–24). All members are to have "the same care for one another," and suffer and rejoice together (vv. 25–26). The body that Paul talks about has apostles, prophets, and teachers ruling and guiding it (vv. 28–29). This is not a description of the invisible church, but of the visible, and in this context it appears that the baptism Paul speaks of is also a visible baptism. What brings us into the visible body of Christ is the visible rite of baptism, through which the Spirit works to join us as members of that body.

At least, the Reformed theologians who compiled the proof texts to the Westminster Confession thought so, since they used 1 Corinthians 12:13 as a proof text for the claim that baptism is given "for the solemn admission of the party baptized into the visible church" (28.1). The overall context in the Confession makes it clear that this is talking about incorporation into the visible church. The "body" into which one is baptized by the Spirit is made up of slaves and freemen. There is no hint that it is anything but the visible church, and the entry into the visible church is indeed the water and Spirit of baptism.

Baptism for the Dead

In 1 Corinthians 15:29, Paul argues for the reality of resurrection with two disorienting rhetorical questions: "Otherwise, what will those do who are baptized for the dead? If the dead are not raised at all, why then are they baptized for them?"

What does Paul mean by "baptize" in this passage? Most commentators believe he refers to a water rite. There is little dispute about this, though Jerome Murphy-O'Connor suggests it is a metaphor for "being destroyed." In his view, Paul is asking rhetorically why preachers ("they") are being destroyed ("baptized") for the sake of those who lack wisdom ("the dead"). Though this interpretation makes some sense of the connection between verse 29 and the following verses, it hardly fits the language of verse 29. Any interpretation that requires inverted commas for all the key words is, to put it mildly, suspect. Apart from the idiosyncratic Murphy-O'Connor, no one seems to doubt that here "baptize" means baptize.

The interesting question in 1 Corinthians 15:29 is not what "baptize" means but what "for the dead" means. Mormons and many others have taken this passage as evidence that some in the early church baptized living people as surrogates for the unbaptized dead, a practice that continued in some heretical groups into the patristic period. Didymus the Blind, for instance, claims that "The Marcionites baptize the living on behalf of dead unbelievers, not knowing that baptism saves only the person who receives it." Chrysostom offers a more colorful description in his fortieth homily on 1 Corinthians: "When any Catechumen departs among them [Marcionites], having concealed the living man under the couch of the dead, they approach the corpse and talk with him, and ask him if he wishes to receive baptism; then when he makes no answer, he that is concealed underneath saith in his stead that of course he should wish to be baptized; and so they baptize him instead of the departed, like men jesting upon the stage"—the stage being for Chrysostom that than which nothing worse can be conceived.

Other early documents show that baptism was not only performed *for* the dead, but sometimes *on* them. (The era of baptizing house pets and farm animals was still some centuries away.) Baptism of corpses was apparently widespread enough in North Africa that the Code of the African Churches, compiled from various councils and approved in 419, included a canon condemning the practice: "Neither the Eucharist nor Baptism should be given to the bodies of the dead." In a Greek version of the canon, this explanation is added: "For it is written: 'Take, Eat,' but the bodies of the dead can neither 'take' nor 'eat.'" That's hard to argue with.

Calvin challenged this line of interpretation, pointing out that "it is hard to believe that people who were denying the resurrection were at one and the same time making use of a rite like this," since the rite makes little sense unless it is done with a view to resurrection. If the Corinthians denying the resurrection were not the same Corinthians who were baptizing the dead, they could respond to Paul's criticism with "Why do you put pressure on us with this old wives' superstition, when in fact you do not approve of it yourself?" And if Paul disapproved of the practice, why didn't he say so? He was not one to shrink from confrontation, particularly with the Corinthians.

If his argument is to work, Paul must be appealing to a practice that both he and the Corinthians accept as legitimate. If the Corinthians do not "baptize for the dead," then Paul's appeal to this practice is useless. If Paul doesn't think the dead should be baptized, then his Corinthian opponents have a ready-made and decisive rejoinder.

So, what is "baptism for the dead"? Calvin suggests that "for the dead" means "those regarded as dead already," in other words, the mortally ill. Paul's argument is: What's the use of death-bed baptisms if there is no resurrection? Perhaps. But Chrysostom suggests a more plausible line of argument. The baptismal rite of his time included a confession of faith in the resurrection: "I believe in the resurrection of the dead." Thus, "with a view to this art thou baptized, the resurrection of thy dead body, believing that it no longer remains dead." Baptism is added to the creed as a sign to assure the baptized. Citing Romans 6, Chrysostom says that entering the water and emerging from it "is a symbol of the descent into Hades and return thence" (*Homily 40 on 1 Corinthians*). Baptism for the dead is not a bizarre perversion of baptism. All Christian baptisms are baptisms for the dead, for everyone comes to the font dead in trespasses and sins. This also fits with the following verses, which show that Paul, having been baptized in hope of resurrection, faces danger, strives with beasts, and sacrifices himself for the church.

This almost satisfies. But not quite. Paul uses a distancing third person—"they" baptize for the dead. Why not "we"? Paul might well be referring to Jewish practices. Under the ceremonial laws of Torah, every washing was a washing "for the dead" (cf. Num. 19). Uncleanness was a ceremonial form of death, and through washings of various sorts the unclean dead were restored to life in fellowship with Yahweh (Lev. 15). Paul might be emphasizing that even Jewish washings of the old covenant were performed in hope of a better resurrection.

Whatever the particulars of Paul's argument, one thing is clear from 1 Corinthians 15:29: "Baptism" means baptism.

Clothed in Christ

James D. G. Dunn, retired professor of New Testament at Durham, claims to be part of a small minority of commentators who do not believe Paul was referring to water baptism in Galatians 3:27. So let's start with him.

In his 1970 book, *Baptism in the Holy Spirit*, Dunn suggests that the phrase "baptized into" is a "metaphor drawn from the rite of baptism" that describes "the entry of the believer into the spiritual relationship of the Christian with Christ" or the "spiritual transformation which makes one a Christian." Paul's reference to "clothing" is metaphorical, and therefore "baptized" must also be metaphorical—as if Paul could not write both literally and metaphorically in one sentence. Further, Dunn says, Galatians as a whole deals with the contrast between a "relationship with God . . . through the law and which is entered by an outward, physical rite" and the new covenant relationship "through the Spirit of Christ and which is entered by the act of believing." Since Paul has spent so much of the letter polemicizing against finding identity through a physical rite, he could hardly be expected to return to a different physical rite here. Paul does not challenge the Jews by saying, "Your rites are ineffective, but ours are effective," but instead points "to the cross and resurrection, to faith and the Spirit." Anyone who focuses on the baptismal rite itself is like a child who "remembers the illustration but pays too little heed to the moral drawn from it."

To that I am tempted to repeat something I heard somewhere: Become like a little child.

But perhaps a counter-argument or two is necessary. For starters, Dunn to the contrary, Paul does not describe the shift from the Old to New as a simple shift from external to internal. He reminds the Galatians, after all, that they received the Spirit through "hearing with faith" (3:2), that is, through the physical act of preaching. He teaches that Christ has been slaughtered as a Passover Lamb (1 Cor. 5:7), but he immediately follows with an exhortation to keep a new covenant feast (5:8). The new Israel as much as the old celebrates an actual Passover feast, with physical food, manducation, and drinking. Dunn would admit that Paul instructs Christians to be baptized, but what's the use of that if "outward physical rites" are characteristic of the Old Law? Further, the phrase "baptized into Christ" may be a shortened version of the phrase "baptize in the name" (Acts 2:38; 8:16; 10:48; 19:5; 1 Cor. 1:13, 15). Since there is an allusion to the baptismal formula here, Paul is talking about the rite of water baptism.

More importantly, it's essential to see how baptism fits into Paul's argument in Galatians. Paul's letter is not primarily about individual soteriology, but about the union of Jews and Gentiles in the one new man, Jesus the Christ, and the coming of a new creation through His death and resurrection. Paul opens the letter charging that the Galatians have abandoned the gospel he preached to them, but in the opening chapter he does not explicitly state what that gospel is nor how the Galatians have distorted it. We get a hint of the problem in 2:11–16, where Paul recounts how he excoriated Peter for refusing to eat with Gentiles (v. 12), which, from Paul's perspective, amounted to a denial of justification by faith (v. 16). Paul finally gets to the heart of his rebuke in 3:1–5: The issue is whether the Spirit comes through the "works of the law" or through hearing the gospel with faith. If the Spirit comes to those who believe the gospel, then they must be "perfected" in the same manner and refuse the temptation to return to the "fleshly" ordinances of the Law (3:3).

Paul then launches into a review of redemptive history, showing that the Law was nestled within the promise. By bringing Israel under a curse, Torah was the paradoxical means for bringing the Spirit to those who share the faith of Abraham (3:6–14). What was the purpose of the Law, then? Paul says here that it was given as a temporary "paedagogue" that kept Israel in custody until "faith" came (3:19, 23–24). In Galatians, the good news is that the promise to Abraham has been fulfilled; through Jesus, God has kept the pre-evangel promise that "all the nations shall be blessed in you" (3:8). Faith has come, and the Jews and Gentiles who believe in Jesus are no longer under a tutor, nor under the "elementary principles" that governed the world in its infancy (4:1–7).

This is the context for Paul's claims in 3:26–29. All those who share the faith of Abraham are "sons of God" (v. 26), that is, true Israelites (cf. Exod. 4:23). Whether they are of Jewish or Gentile origin, whether they are of slave or free class, whether they are male or female, they are all heirs of the inheritance promised to Abraham, the promise of the Spirit (vv. 28–29). The context for verse 27 is thus all about the formation of a new community of Abraham's seed. Baptism into Christ and being clothed with Christ is thus all about incorporation into membership in this new body, the body that is "one in Christ Jesus" (v. 28), the community of those who "are Christ's" (v. 29). Galatians has to do with the re-mapping of Israel and the church that occurs in the death and resurrection of Jesus. It is talking about the formation of a new historical body.

That new body is strikingly different from the old. In the Old Covenant system, only members of the covenant people were circumcised, and even God-fearing Gentiles remain uncircumcised. Circumcision distinguished between Jew and Gentile, and also between male and female. In the New Covenant, baptism is applied indiscriminately to all who believe—whether Jew or Gentile, slave or free, male or female. Baptism thus symbolizes and enacts the union of Jew and Gentile in the church, ritually marking all the baptized as sons of Abraham.

A reference to the rite of baptism fits the logic of Paul's argument in a way that a reference to some profound spiritual experience doesn't. The argument as a whole suggests Paul is identifying a rite that marks a new people, the Abrahamic people.

One Baptism

A similar argument can be made for the use of "baptism" in Ephesians 4. The phrase "one baptism" occurs in a list of the sevenfold unity of the church (v. 5). The church is "one body" governed and controlled by "one Spirit" who inspired "one hope." It is under "one Lord," confesses "one faith," and is marked by "one baptism" to worship "one God and Father of all" (vv. 4–6). As Paul goes on, he emphasizes the diversity of gifts within the unified community of believers (vv. 7–11), diverse gifts given so that the church will be built up into full maturity in Christ Jesus, as "each individual part" contributes to the "growth of the body for the building up of itself in love" (v. 16).

The unity-and-diversity theme is connected to Paul's discussion of the church in Romans 12 and 1 Corinthians 12. Jesus' gifts to the church are "apostles, prophets, evangelists, pastors and teachers" (v. 11), and this makes it clear that Paul is talking about the historical community of believers, not some invisible heavenly people nor some sub-section of the visible church. This context suggests Paul is talking about the visible "one baptism" that marks the visible church.

The larger context of Paul's argument supports this interpretation as well. The argument begins in chapter 2, where Paul announces and explains the character of the new people of God, in which Gentiles who were once at a distance from God are brought near and united with the Jews in God's new household, built up as a new temple (2:11–22). Paul is clearly describing the historical communities of Israel and the church, and he emphasizes the union of the human race into "one new man" (2:15) united by "one Spirit" (2:18) to approach the Father.

In chapter 3, Paul begins to exhort the Ephesians to live out the unity the gospel announces: "For this reason I, Paul, the prisoner of Christ Jesus for the sake of you Gentiles," he opens (3:1). But the reference to Paul's ministry to the Gentiles leads him into a digression on his particular role in the reunion of the human race in Christ. He is a "steward" ("economist," v. 1) or "minister" (deacon, v. 7) of the mystery of God, the mystery that consists in the incorporation of Gentiles as co-heirs, body-parts, sharers in the promise (3:1–6). He returns to the exhortation at the beginning of chapter 4, repeating some of the language from 3:1: "I, therefore, the prisoner of the Lord, entreat you to walk in a manner worthy of the calling to which you have been called." The calling to which the church is called is a calling to unity, the call to live as the unified people of God, knit together from Jews and Gentiles. To accomplish this requires "humility and gentleness, with patience, showing forbearance to one another in love, being diligent to preserve the unity of the Spirit in the bond of peace" (4:2–3).

Given the flow of Paul's argument, it's clear that he's talking about the historical community of the church, which consists of people from every tribe and tongue and nation and people. Because God has gathered such a diverse collection of human beings into one household, there are bound to be tensions, strife, rivalries, conflicts. Living the unity to which we are called will demand forbearance, humility, patience, and love. These exhortations again assume that Paul is talking about the actual flesh-and-blood "mixed multitude" of the visible church.

In this context, Paul's list enumerates the seven unities of the church. The unity of the church is ultimately grounded in the unity of the Triune God. Jesus prayed the church would be one "even as" the Father, Son, and Spirit are one (Jn. 17), and Paul describes the church the same way: The one body is united by "one Spirit," "one Lord" Jesus, and "one God and Father" (Eph. 4:4–6). That unity in Father, Son, and Spirit cannot be perceived, except by faith, and it is the most fundamental reality and source of the unity of the church. But this invisible unity comes to expression in one confessed faith and one hope, and it is visibly marked by the fact that the members of the church all share in one baptism. Whether Jew or Greek, slave or free, male or female, African or Asian, Irish or English, Croat or Serb, they all have entered the body and become members of that body through the same event, the one water baptism they all share.

Sharing the Circumcision of Christ

Colossians 2:12 refers to a baptism through or in which we have been buried with Christ, raised through faith in the God who raises the dead. Verse 13 goes on to describe the difference this baptismal burial-and-resurrection has on the lives of those who receive it: "When you were dead in your transgression and the uncircumcision of your flesh, He made you alive together with Him, having forgiven all our transgression, having canceled the certificate of debt consisting of decrees against us and which was hostile to us" (vv. 13–14a). The imagery is difficult and debated, but Paul clearly implies that the baptismal event, whatever it was, raised the dead to new life, granted forgiveness of sins, and canceled debt.

But what was the baptismal event? Is this baptism water baptism or some overwhelming spiritual event, conversion or something like it?

Several points favor the conclusion that "baptism" means baptism here. First, Paul uses language similar to what he used in Romans 6, linking baptism to burial and new life with Christ. Above, I argued that Paul was talking about water baptism in Romans 6, and the similarity of language indicates that he is talking about the same rite here. Second, the flow of thought supports the idea that Paul is referring to water baptism. He is challenging the Jewish use of circumcision as a tribal badge and claims instead that the true circumcision is one done "without hands," that is, by God Himself (2:11). What is needed is not merely a stripping off of the foreskin but an entire "stripping of the flesh," the flesh of Adamic humanity. This is accomplished not by the ritual of circumcision but by the "circumcision of Christ," which is best understood as a reference to His death in the flesh on the cross. This interpretation of the phrase leads neatly into the references to burial and resurrection in verse 12. Jesus' final work is all summarized here: His circumcision on the cross, His burial, and His resurrection. It is Jesus' circumcision that undoes the "uncircumcision" of the Colossians and truly removes the flesh from them.

What flesh is removed by the circumcision of Christ on the cross? This has often been interpreted as the sinful nature that we inherit from Adam, and that is certainly a central meaning of "flesh" in the New Testament. Yet, the word also has more concrete, cultural connotations in various passages. When Paul lists all the things that might give him "confidence in the flesh" (Phil. 3:4), he mentions circumcision, his Hebrew heritage, his devotion to the law, his zeal, and his obedience (vv. 4–6). Boasting in any of these things would be a form of boasting in "the flesh." Flesh includes everything that is Paul's by virtue of his Jewish birth, his circumcision in the flesh, and his Jewish training and heritage. All his cultural inheritance is flesh, and so much *skubalon*, "dung," in comparison to Christ (v. 8). When Paul was baptized, then, he put off the flesh of his Jewishness and became a different man, Christ's man.

Adamic nature is lived out in particular cultural identities, habits of conduct, ideas, rituals, markings, values. This whole complex of ideas, practices, symbols, and stories may, in Pauline terms, be categorized as the flesh that must be abandoned if one is to follow Christ. Paul, in fact, wants the Gentile Philippians to "join in following my example" of renunciation (Phil. 3:17). Roman citizens have to be ready to renounce their rights. Philosophically trained Greeks will have to consider Plato and Aristotle so much rubbish for the sake of Christ. The Greco-Roman in the street will have to be ready to put off the flesh of his inherited ways and manners and prejudices to be joined to Christ in His body.

Back to Colossians 2:12: Paul says the flesh of sinful nature, and the cultural forms that Adamic humanity takes, are stripped away in the circumcision of Christ on Calvary's tree. Jesus remakes a humanity that is not subjected to these fleshly forms of life, but instead is led by the Spirit. God Himself, without hands, strips the flesh from each believer through the Spirit of the crucified Son. Verse 12 specifically fits into this argument by referring to the way that we come to share in that new humanity which has been stripped of flesh. Verse 12 shows how individuals come to share in

Jesus' "circumcision without hands," how we come to share in the death, burial, and resurrection of Jesus. Specifically, it tells us how Gentiles who are uncircumcised in the flesh come to be circumcised. They are circumcised, made alive, and forgiven by sharing in the burial and resurrection of Jesus, and they share in this by water baptism.

Through baptism, the story of Jesus' circumcision, burial and resurrection becomes ours. Tribesmen who grew up looking back to their ancestors gain a new past in Jesus. Citizens who identify with the "in" group of their city become members of a new city. Together, in the One New Man, those who share in the circumcision of Christ by baptism move into a new future, knowing that Jesus has stripped the rulers and authorities that appeared to be stripping Him, exposed their emptiness, and triumphed over them on the cross.

Conclusion

It appears, then, that in the New Testament "baptism" means baptism. When Paul in particular uses the word "baptize," he is referring to the water rite that initiates the baptized into the fellowship of the church. If that's true, then we must face up to all the passages quoted at the beginning of this chapter and recognize that the Bible attributes an astonishing power to this water initiation. How are we to understand this? The answer becomes clearer when, in chapter 3, we examine the second of my propositions: "The body of Christ" is the body of Christ.

3

The "Body of Christ" is the Body of Christ

In the last chapter, I suggested that the biblical teaching on baptismal efficacy can be summarized in three axioms:

1. *"Baptism" is baptism. When the New Testament writers use the word "baptism," they normally mean the water rite of entry into the church.*
2. *"The body of Christ" is the body of Christ. When the New Testament writers call the church the "body of Christ," they mean the visible or historical church is the body of Christ.*
3. *Apostasy happens.*

The second axiom is the critical one in all the current debates within the Reformed churches about baptism. The question in dispute is not baptismal efficacy *per se*. No one in the Reformed world says there's magic in the water, and virtually no one anywhere, even the most Catholic of Catholics, believes that baptism eternally and invariably saves everyone who gets wet. The question has to do with the significance of baptismal entry into the visible church and, behind this, with the question of what the visible church is.

Let's start slow. All parties in these Reformed debates agree that baptism admits the baptized into the visible church. Such is the explicit teaching of Westminster Confession of Faith (28.1), which says that baptism is, among other things, "for the solemn admission of the party baptized into the visible church." Continental Reformed confessions teach the same: Through baptism "we are received into the Church of God, and separated from all other people and strange religions" (*Belgic Confession*, Article 34), and baptized infants are "included in the covenant and church of God" and thereby "distinguished from the children of unbelievers" (*Heidelberg Catechism* #74). The *Second Helvetic Confession* echoes this: "to be baptized in the name of Christ is to be enrolled, entered, and received into the covenant and family, and so into the inheritance, of the sons of God" (chapter XX).

The dispute is about what this means. What does a baptized person become a member *of* when he becomes a member of the church? What kind of bond to *Christ*, and through Him to the Father and Spirit, is forged when one enters the visible church by baptism? Can we say that a member of the church is, necessarily, a member of *Christ*? Answers to these questions depend on ecclesiological assumptions, on the answer to our question, Is the visible church the body of Christ? If the visible church *is* the body of Christ, and if the body of Christ is the community united to the humanity of the Son of God by the Spirit, then baptism joins the baptized to Christ the Son. If the visible church is something less than this, then baptism is of course something less too.

One might think these questions are answerable with a straightforward syllogism:

1. *Baptism admits the baptized to the church.*
2. *The church is the body of Christ.*
3. *Therefore, baptism admits the baptized to the body of Christ.*

To see what the current debates are all about, it's worth pausing to reflect that the Reformed tradition has been ambiguous about this syllogism as it stands.

Specifically, the Reformed tradition has been ambiguous about premise #2. The Westminster Confession distinguishes between the "invisible" church, which it describes as "the spouse, the body, the fullness of him that fills all in all" (25.1) and the "visible" church, which is described as "the kingdom of the Lord Jesus Christ, the house and family of God" (25.2). Note the distinction between the intimate language of section 1 and the more legal, political language of section 2. The invisible church is the church in intimate union with Christ—the church that is bride and body and fullness. The visible church is a society, a kingdom, a household or family, an external social reality. Baptism admits to the second, but not necessarily the first.

Those who appended the Scripture proofs believed that the *visible* church is the body of Christ, because they included 1 Corinthians 12:12 among the Scripture texts concerning the visible church. Further, the Larger Catechism (#167) says that we improve on our baptism in part by striving "to walk in brotherly love, as being baptized by the same Spirit into one body," and "body" in this answer is surely the visible church. Yet, the Confession itself restricts "body" language to the invisible church. In this view, of course, baptism does *not* (or not necessarily) join the baptized to the body of Christ, since there is no guarantee that the baptized person is a member of the invisible church. The baptized are members of the kingdom and household of God, but only the baptized elect are, strictly, members of the body of Christ.

Given the distinction between the intimate invisible church and the legal visible church, the syllogism gets interrupted. At best, a question mark overshadows it:

1. *Baptism admits the baptized to the visible church.*
2. *But the visible church is not the body of Christ. At least, there's no direct identification of body and visible church.*
3. *Therefore baptism doesn't admit the baptized to the body of Christ. Or, we don't know whether it does or not.*

This confessional ambiguity is founded on and has produced persistent dualities within Reformed theology, which are evident most clearly in various formulas concerning the "dual aspect of the covenant." As Louis Berkhof summarizes, Reformed theologians have distinguished between an internal and external covenant, the essence of the covenant and its administration, a conditional and absolute covenant, and the covenant as a legal relationship and as a communion of life. Working with these dualisms, one might reformulate the syllogism along these lines:

1. *Baptism admits the baptized to the visible church.*
2. *The visible church involves an external, conditional, and legal covenant relationship with God.*
3. *Therefore, baptism admits the baptized into an external, conditional, legal relationship with God.*

This would be fine if it were what the New Testament says. But it's not. The New Testament does not describe the church as a community that is united to Christ in purely external and legal ways. The New Testament applies the language of intimacy to the visible church while the Westminster Confession confines it to the invisible church. What *does* the New Testament say? It says, "*All* were baptized into Moses in the cloud and in the sea" (1 Cor. 10:2), and likewise "by one Spirit we were *all* baptized *into one body*" (1 Cor. 12:13). And, more fundamentally, it asks, "Has Christ been divided?" (1 Cor. 1:13).

At this point, these are assertions. I must demonstrate them. But first, we need to consider . . .

The Alternative

Suppose the "body of Christ" is *not* the body of Christ? To put it more precisely, what if the historical, visible, empirical church is not really the people united as members to the Incarnate Son by the Spirit of the Father? What if it's no more than a legal and external community, a pointer to the *real* body of Christ, which is invisible? What if the *real* body of Christ never appears as such in history? What then?

Then, to paraphrase Paul, is our hope vain. Then we are most to be pitied. Then is our faith useless, and our preaching false.

Strong claim, that. Can I justify it? Does the truth of the gospel depend on claiming that the historical, visible, empirical church is the people united as members to the Incarnate Son by the Spirit of the Father?

I submit that it does, but I want to qualify carefully. I am not saying that people who disagree with me on this point are not Christians, or that they are preaching what Paul would call "another gospel." But I am saying there is systematic ambiguity and inconsistency within any theology that denies or hedges on, overtly or by implication, the confession that the body of Christ is not a historical phenomenon. This systematic ambiguity and inconsistency creates dissonance in our preaching of the gospel, robs the gospel of some degree of its power, and ultimately undermines the claims the gospel makes.

To make the case, we need to go back to the beginning, to the garden. God's purpose in Adam was to form a race on earth that would worship Him in truth and subdue and rule the earth in faithful obedience to Him. God intended to lead Adam's race to maturity, from glory to glory. Sin interrupted and presented an obstacle to that purpose, but sin didn't change God's purpose. From the first gospel promise to Adam and Eve outside Eden, through Abraham and the patriarchs, Moses and the exodus, the judges and kings, to the final climactic act of salvation in Jesus, God's purpose has been the same: He was going to deal with sin in order to form a race on earth that will worship Him in truth and subdue and rule the earth in faithful obedience to Him.

The good news of the gospel is that God has, at long last, acted in His Son to achieve this purpose. Through the work of the Son and the gift of the Spirit, Israel's heart of stone (the tablets of Moses) has been replaced by a living heart of flesh so that the new Israel "will be careful to observe My ordinances" (Ezek. 36:27). The new Israel, cleansed by the Son and renewed by the Spirit, turns the desolate land into a garden and ruins into fortified cities (Ezek. 36:33–36).

If there is no new Israel on earth, if the visible church is only *kind of* a new Israel, then the gospel is simply not true—because the gospel is precisely that there *is* a new Israel, Jesus Himself, and in Him a new people of God. And, the new Israel is precisely the people indwelt by the Spirit. If that description—an Israel indwelt by the Spirit—doesn't describe any actually existing, historical community of people, then the gospel is false.

Or, try it this way: Genesis 1 says we are created in the image of a God who speaks of Himself in the plural, a God who can not only say "I" but "we." We are created as social beings, entangled with the lives of others and with the things of the world in such profound ways that it's often difficult to know where one ends and another begins. A woman loses her husband of fifty years and feels that she's lost part of herself. A burglar empties a home, and the owners feel raped. People get attached to places—to rocks, trees, soil, topography—and feel disoriented when they move to a new place.

Because of the way human beings are made, sin damages our relations with each other and the world as much as it damages our relationship with God. Like Adam, we blame other people to assuage our guilt; like Cain, we butcher them because their deeds are righteous and ours are wicked. We employ our tools and goods to destroy rather than to build.

Given the way God created us, salvation for the human race *must* take a social form. Were God to save individuals from within the human race and restore them to individual fellowship with Himself, He would not be saving human beings as they were created. He would be saving "egos" but not creatures who say "we." If He delivered us from individual sins without delivering us from the sinful ways we treat one another and the world, He would not be saving us from sin at all. If God is going to restore the human race to right order, He must form a society of the saved. If God were to delay the formation of this race until the end of time, then salvation would be delayed until the end of time. If there is no society of the saved in history, then there simply is no salvation in history. Salvation is still a distant, longed-for possibility. If salvation doesn't take form in history, a *social* form in history, the gospel is untrue. If there is no community of the saved, salvation has not actually occurred at all.

On the other hand, if salvation has occurred, it must have a visible, historical form. And it has, and the name of that visible, historical form of salvation is "church" or "body of Christ." Of course, salvation-in-social-form, that is, the church as the body of Christ, is not yet perfected. There are false sons in her pale, and each member remains sinful and immature. Imperfect as it is, however, salvation-in-social-form is a reality now, so that the "body of Christ" is truly the body of Christ.

If this is not true, if the church is not this new Israel according to the Spirit, if she is not directly and literally the seed of Abraham in the Seed of Abraham, then is our faith vain; then are we most to be pitied.

The "Body of Christ" Is the Visible Church

So, we know what the stakes are. But what do the Scriptures say? Do the Scriptures use the phrase "body of Christ" to refer to the "visible" church, the elect within the visible church, or the elect in general?

Before looking at the New Testament, let me register a qualification concerning the way we talk about the church. Reformed theology has frequently "spatialized" the church, conceiving of it as two overlapping communities, the "visible" and the "invisible," which can be diagrammed as concentric circles, the invisible being the inner circle within the shell of the visible. That certainly captures some of the reality of the church, since it highlights the fact that not everyone who is part of the historical community of believers will finally be saved. There are hypocrites and false sons and temporary members within the body of Christ, and they will slip away, be cut off, or be denounced at the final judgment.

Yet, this spatialized model has sometimes been understood in a way that undermines the reality of the visible church. This spatialized model can lead us to deny that the church in time, the mixed and imperfect church, is the church of Jesus Christ, His people. This visible church, for some, is only *kind of* the church of Jesus Christ.

To avoid this problem, I prefer to use the terms "historical" and "eschatological" to describe the church. What we know today is not a "visible" church but a "historical" church; what we will know at the end of history is not an "invisible" but an "eschatological" church. This significantly changes, and simplifies, the question we need to address to the New Testament writers. When we frame the question as "Is Paul or Peter or John talking about the visible or invisible church?" we tie ourselves in knots. How can we tell whether Paul is addressing the elect within the church or the whole church? We can't.

But when we ask, "Is John or Peter or Paul talking about the historical or the eschatological church?" it's a question we can answer. Any passage that deals with a church that is a mixed community; any passage that describes the structures, institutions, and government of the church; any passage that deals with the rites and ceremonies of the church is about the historical church, the empirical community of believers made up of local communities of believers.

With this in mind, we can turn to the New Testament, where we find that "body of Christ" does have a range of referents. In some contexts, the "body" is the humanity, and particularly the physical body, of Jesus (Heb. 10:10; 1 Pet. 2:24; apparently, 1 Cor. 7:4). The phrase can also refer to the bread of the Eucharist (1 Cor. 11:14; apparently, 1 Cor. 10:16). But I submit there is only one place where the word "body" with reference to the church might possibly refer to the eschatological body of the elect—Ephesians 1:23. That's not certain, but it's possible in the context of Ephesians 1, which famously includes several references to God's eternal predestination of sons in the Beloved Son. Otherwise, when it refers to a communion of people, "body of Christ" refers, quite straightforwardly, to a visible, historical community of professing believers.

In Romans 12, for instance, Paul compares the community of Christians to the human body: "Just as we have many members in one body and all the members do not have the same function, so we, who are many, are one body in Christ" (vv. 4–5). The diversity of the body, as Paul develops the image, is a diversity of ministries, as each member of the body acts "according to the grace given to us" (v. 6). The body he's talking about is a body with servants, teachers, exhorters, givers, leaders, and those involved in mercy ministries (vv. 7–8). If this sounds a little like your home church, there's a reason: Paul is describing a community very much like your home church. The church Paul describes is just as visible, just as cramped with problems, just as bumbling as it confronts crises and changes—be it First Baptist or Berea Bible or St. Anthony's Episcopal or any other church in your town. And—importantly—Paul calls this group of mutual servants the "body of Christ."

Paul makes much the same point in 1 Corinthians 12.[8] Again, the image of the body is an image of oneness-in-manyness: "as the body is one and yet has many members, and all the members of the body, though they are many, are one body, so also is Christ" (v. 12). As in Romans 12, the diversity is a diversity of gifts: wisdom, knowledge, faith, healing, miracles, prophecy, discernment of spirits, tongues, interpretation of tongues (vv. 8–10). It's the "body" where there are apostles, prophets, teachers, miracles, healings, helps, administrations, tongues (v. 28). It's the body that has greater and lesser members, seemly and unseemly organs (v. 22–23). It's the body in which the members cannot stand alone, but depend on other organs (v. 21). It's the body whose members must strive for unity (v. 25). It's the body where individual members suffer and receive honor, rejoice and weep, and where all the members share in the glories and humiliations of each (v. 26).

Here Paul emphasizes that the unity of the diverse body is guaranteed by the work of the Spirit, the "same Spirit" who "works all these things" (v. 11). Behind all the fervent, sometimes fevered, work of the church's members is the powerful working of the Spirit. Again, Paul could be describing your church—provided, of course, you attend a church where there's speaking in tongues and interpretation. More seriously, Paul is clearly describing a visible community of believers who all devote their energies and spiritual gifts to the "common good" (v. 7).

---

8. It's one of those happy mnemonic providences that Romans and 1 Corinthians both deal with this issue in chapter 12.

First Corinthians 12:12 is particularly striking for the way Paul identifies the Head-and-members body of Christ as "Christ." "Christ" is not just the title of the Anointed Head. The anointing flows like the dew of Hermon down from our priestly Head, down the beard, down to the skirts of the garments. Whoever is touched by that anointing in the Spirit (vv. 12–13) becomes a member of the body of the Head. Whoever is touched by that anointing is part of "Christ." Together, Anointed Head and anointed body make a single Anointed One, one Christ. Augustine's idea of a *totus Christus*, a "whole Christ" made of Head and body is not a fanciful fabrication of a Plotinian mind. It is purely Pauline. And this "whole Christ" is the visible, historical church.

A bit earlier in 1 Corinthians, Paul refers to the corporate body of Christ in connection with the Eucharist. It's not clear whether 1 Corinthians 10:16's reference to "sharing in the body of Christ" means sharing in Christ's personal body or the corporate body. But in verse 17, "one body" clearly refers to the corporate body of the church, since Paul uses the same many-and-one formula he uses in Romans 12 and 1 Corinthians 12. Now, is this one-and-many body the body of the eternally elect, or the historical body of the church? The opening and closing clauses of verse 17 make the answer plain: The "one body" is constituted by a common sharing in "one loaf." The "one body" of 10:17 is the community that shares the Eucharistic meal at the Lord's table. Those who receive the "one body" *are* the "one body."

In Ephesians, Paul refers to the church as the "body of Christ" at several points: 2:16 speaks of the reconciliation of Jew and Gentile into "one body to God through the cross" (v. 15). This clearly refers to the first-century community that consisted of both Jews and Gentiles, slaves and freemen, men and women (cf. 3:6). Paul's whole point in this section of the letter highlights how the gospel sutures together a humanity cut in half by circumcision. Once separated, excluded, and estranged, Gentiles are now united, included, and fellow citizens with the saints. The distant Gentiles are brought near to God in Jesus (vv. 13–19). That process is *the* crucial (in every sense) governmental and "social" concern of the first-century church. It's not, however, primarily a concern about the salvation of individual Gentiles, since Gentiles had been saved as soon as Gentiles came into existence (Gen. 14). Paul is dealing with the organization of the visible, historical community of the church, and this he describes as the "one body."

Ephesians 4:4–16 is even more clearly about the visible church. The "one body" of which Paul talks in that chapter is marked by "one baptism" (v. 5) and is built up through the gifts of the ascended Christ—gifts such as apostles, prophets, evangelists, pastors, and teachers (v. 11). It's a body of "holy ones" engaged in the ministry (v. 12), maturing from childhood toward adulthood, straining for the "measure of the stature which belongs to the fullness of Christ" (v. 13). It is a growing church, a church under construction, a church aiming to become like Jesus, her Head (vv. 14–15). And this church-in-progress Paul describes as "one body" (v. 4), the "body of Christ" (v. 12), "the whole body" that has Christ as its head (vv. 15–16). None of this makes sense if Paul is talking about the eschatological church, the elect. They are not growing up into mature Godlikeness, but have already arrived. This is clearly a church in progress, not a church come to its destination.

In the previous chapter, I alluded to the Trinitarian structure of Paul's description of the unity of the church in Ephesians 4. Intertwined with his heptamerous description of the church's unity is the name of the Triune God, moving in the reverse of baptismal order from Spirit to Son to Father. Through the outpouring of the One Spirit, the church is conformed to the One Lord and given access to One Father. The church is the unified body related in Triune ways to the Triune God.

For my purposes, the important thing about this Trinitarian structure is that Paul uses it to describe the unified *visible* church. It's not only the eschatological, invisible church of the elect that can be described as being united by one Spirit, ruled by one Lord, on a journey toward one Father. This is a description of the *historical* church. The visible church is united together by its union with the Triune God, by its unity in the Spirit with the Son of the Father. If this is what the visible church *is*, then it would seem impossible for membership in the visible church to be merely "legal" or merely "external." It would seem impossible for "political" and "legal" categories to fully describe the character of the church. The *visible* church is the body that is united to the Triune God, and membership in her means participation in the fellowship of the Triune God.

Finally, Paul uses the image of the "body" several times in Colossians. Jesus is the Alpha Creator who holds the creation together and the personal Logos who performs the function the abstract impersonal Logos often played in Greek philosophy (1:16–17). Verse 1:18 goes on to describe Him as the "head of the body" who is the "beginning, the firstborn from the dead." Though the referent of "body" here is not explicit, the similarity between Colossians 1:20 and Ephesians 2:11–22 ("reconciliation" and "peace") suggests that Paul is talking about the combined Jew-Gentile community of the first-century church. Later in the chapter, Paul directly identifies the "body" as "the church" (1:24). In that context, the church refers to the historical church in which Paul ministers and for which Paul suffers (vv. 24–25). Colossians 2:19 emphasizes the connection between the body and the head, extending the analogy between church and body by talking about joints, ligatures, and the growth of the body. Though the referent of "body" is somewhat ambiguous here, the similarity to the extended analogy that Paul employs in 1 Corinthians 12 argues for a reference to the visible church. In 1 Corinthians 12, Paul speaks of organs and members that contribute to the health of the whole body, and here he speaks of ligatures and joints. Calvin surely understood Colossians 2:19 as a reference to the visible church, since he used the imagery of joints and ligaments to explain the necessity of a pastoral office for the health of the church.

A final body reference occurs in Colossians 3:15, where Paul exhorts the Colossians as the "chosen of God, holy and beloved" to "compassion, kindness, humility, gentleness and patience" (3:12–13). They are to bear with each other's idiosyncracies and irritations, forgiving when there are justified complaints (3:13). All these are means for maintaining love, "the perfect bond of unity" (3:14), the bond that is to characterize the church. This is the "peace of Christ" that must rule the hearts of the Colossians, and to which they are "called." All these exhortations are demanded by the calling of the church to be the "body" (3:15). In context, Paul is clearly exhorting the visible, historical community of believers in Colossae as the "body" of the Lord of peace.

So, "body of Christ" means body of Christ, the historical church. So what? What does it mean to call a gathering of people in history the "body of Christ"? To grasp that, it will be helpful to begin with a consideration of . . .

Jesus' Personal Body

In an effort to summarize all that the Bible teaches about the body of Christ, medieval theologians, building on patristic sources, operated with the theory of the "triple body" of Christ. Jesus has a *personal* body in which He lived and moved during His earthly life. This body is glorified, but not shed, at the resurrection and ascension. Before Jesus left His disciples as a bodily presence, he instituted the Lord's Supper, where the church is offered the *Eucharistic* body of Christ. The community that shares in the Eucharistic body is the *corporate* body of the church, which we have been examining.

Medieval theologians expressed the relations between these different bodies differently. As Henri de Lubac showed in *Corpus Mysticum* (at long last available in English translation), early medieval theologians closely associated the Eucharist with the corporate body. Through His bodily work in the cross and resurrection, Jesus had accomplished salvation, instituted the meal, and founded the church. Now His personal body is invisibly in heaven, and the church gathers and unites together as the corporate body around the Eucharistic feast. For these theologians, it was axiomatic that "the Eucharist makes the church." Participation in the one loaf of the Eucharistic body forms the one corporate body of the church (1 Cor. 10:16–17).

During the high middle ages, this way of understanding the triple body changed. Instead of linking the Eucharistic and corporate bodies, later theologians began tying together the Eucharistic body more closely to the personal body. In place of the earlier model, where sharing the Eucharistic body shaped the corporate body, later medieval theologians were concerned with how the bread of the Eucharist could be turned into the personal body. The late medieval Mass was all about the priest transforming the Eucharistic body into the personal body. Whether the corporate body had any share in this miracle was indifferent. Most Masses in the high middle ages were, in fact, performed without any church present.

Regardless of how the medievals organized these three "bodies," they saw them as inseparably linked. Even the early theologians didn't think the Eucharist or the church could exist without the sacramental presence of the personal body. Only because the Eucharist was a sacrament of the personal body of Jesus could it form the church as the body. And in some way the private Masses of the later middle ages were seen as contributions to the building of the corporate body.

This notion of the triple body helps us to grasp the significance of our earlier conclusion that Paul uses the phrase "body of Christ" to describe the historical church. How is the visible church the body of Christ? What does it mean for Christ to have both a corporate and a personal body?

Let's begin with the personal body. Rudolph Bultmann, for all his heresies, had it right when he observed that in the Bible a man doesn't *have* a body but *is* his body. We touch others, literally and figuratively, through our bodies, but it is indeed *we* who touch *others*. I can talk to my wife because I have a tongue, lungs, a mouth cavity, and vocal chords. She can talk to me because she's wondrously endowed with the same apparatus and, even more miraculously, speaks the same language I do. It's not as if the ghostly inner me uses the tool of my body the way I'd use a microphone. It's not as if my wife's ghostly inner "she" uses the tool of her ears as she would a recorder. If that were the case, I would never actually talk to her; our two ghostly selves would be lonely, shivering selves who have contact with our tools but never with one another. That's not the biblical picture. We have contact with one another not *in spite of* our bodies, but precisely *because of* our bodies. Bodies are not hindrances to communion, but the presupposition of creaturely communion. Souls are united, but only through bodies.

The same goes for our contact with the world. My body touches the world literally and metaphorically, but the contact of my body with the world is *my* contact with the *world*. I know the world through my senses, which all involve bodily operations. Contrary to what many philosophers have said, this doesn't mean we know *only* our sensible impressions. It's not true that all I can know through my bodily senses is the impression of "rectangular brownness" across the room. I know the door through my sense of sight. My bodily senses are my way of having contact with the creation outside me. Phenomenalists and empiricists of all stripes are only disguised Gnostics wishing—with their brains—that they could wish brainlessly, wringing their hands over the tragic realization that they have hands to wring.

Markus Barth puts it well in his commentary on Ephesians: "In Hebrew anthropology the soul is the life kindled by the Spirit which God gave (Gen. 2:7); and man's body is the public *manifestation* of the life that is in man." The Father is one with His Word; the Father and His Image (or manifestation) are one God. Analogously, the soul-flame in man and his bodily manifestation are one man.

What does this have to do with Jesus? The Eternal Son comes into the world in human flesh, with a human body. The Incarnate Son doesn't just *have* a body; He *is* His body. Like your body and my body, Jesus' personal body is the manifestation of the life that is in Him, the life that, in the most precise sense, *is* Him. During Jesus' earthly life, if you wanted to have life, you needed to draw near to the personal body of Jesus. This is precisely what John says at the beginning of his first epistle (1:1–3):

> What was from the beginning, what we have heard, what we have seen with our eyes, what we have looked at and touched with our hands, concerning the Word of Life—and the life was manifested, and we have seen and testify and proclaim to you the eternal life, which was with the Father and was manifested

to us—what we have seen and heard we proclaim to you also, so that you too may have fellowship with us; and indeed our fellowship is with the Father, and with His Son Jesus Christ.

Now, what did John and the apostles (the "we" of this passage) *actually* see and hear and touch? They saw and heard and touched what was there to be seen and heard and touched—namely, the personal body of Jesus. But precisely by seeing the form of Jesus' body, listening as air rushed from His lungs through His vocal chords to be manipulated into words by His lips and tongue, reaching out to touch the nail prints and His pierced side—through all this, they had contact with the "Word of life," with "eternal life" itself. Hearing, seeing, and touching Jesus' human body, they touched, saw, and heard God, because Jesus is His body and because this is the way the Triune God determined to manifest eternal life to us. Through contact with the personal body of Jesus, the apostles had "fellowship" (*koinonia*) with the Father and Son (in the Spirit), and through contact with the apostles, others ("you") come to share in that fellowship.

John is merely summarizing what anyone who watched Jesus for three years could have witnessed for himself. When Jesus spoke in His personal body, the crowds marveled because He spoke with divine authority. In Jesus' bodily presence there was fullness of joy, a continual feast. When His tongue lashed out against the Pharisees and when He physically drove the money-changers from the temple, they were burned with the fire of divine wrath. When a woman with a flow of blood touched His garment, which merely *covered* His body, she was instantly healed, and moments later He raised a young girl by taking her hand. Joy, peace, justice, and power radiated from the Word of life who touched the world in, or better, *as* His human body.

Luther had it exactly right: "This man is God; this God is man."

Ecclesiological Nestorianism

Nestorius couldn't believe this.[9] He couldn't believe that contact with the body of Jesus—so physical, so tangible, so fragile, so mortal—could really be contact with the Word of life. A body made of mud and spit, born, as Augustine said, *inter faeces et urinas*, could not be *that* transparent to divinity. Contact with the body of Jesus was contact with the human nature, but the divine nature kept a safe and respectable distance from the body and the rest of the human nature. Surely, divine nature was not manifested through the body. The divine nature and the human nature walked parallel roads, and sometimes, in great acts of power, momentarily intersected. But the road walked by the man Jesus was not identical to the road of the Son of God.

Nestorianism was surgically (indeed, somewhat savagely) disposed of during the early history of the church. No one wants to be a Christological Nestorian today (though many actually are). Everyone affirms the *Formula of Chalcedon*, which says that the human and divine in Jesus are distinct but not separated.

When we turn from the personal to the corporate body of Jesus, however, Nestorianism is rampant. Here the church (the all-too-human corporate body) is one thing, and the personal presence of the incarnate Word is quite another. Even if we have a visible community of believers faithfully worshiping and serving together, we can't know for sure if this is the body of Christ or if they are joined to Christ. The church walks along one path, Jesus along another; sometimes the paths cross, but we can't say that they are walking the same path. And, more to the point, someone can join a visible community of believers and the corporate body of the Son of God without ever having a bit of real contact with the Son of God Himself. Membership in the church is one thing. That is contact with the "merely legal" or "merely social" body of Christ. Membership

---

9. Nestorius might have. The debate about whether Nestorius was a Nestorian continues, unresolved. I couldn't resolve it if I intended to. For better or worse, however, "Nestorian" is what the church has come to call this particular heresy.

in Christ Himself is quite another thing. Body and Person are detached and work independently.

Hence the Reformed syllogism:

1. *Baptism joins the baptized to the visible church.*
2. *But the visible church is not the body of Christ and is detached from Christ Himself, or at least it is not necessarily attached.*
3. *Therefore, baptism only joins the baptized to the human community of the visible church, but this does not imply any connection with Jesus Himself.*

Immediately the rejoinder: But the union of divine and human in Jesus is unique, unrepeatable, and once-for-all. In Jesus, the Son of God took on full human nature in personal union. The church is not a hypostatic union of divine and human natures.

That rejoinder is perfectly true. The church is *not* another incarnation of the eternal Son of God. The church is *not* hypostatically united to the Son of God. The church is *not* the body of Jesus in the same sense that the personal body of Jesus is the body of Jesus. Yet, the medievals who refused to separate the "bodies" that God joined together have something important to teach us, and that something is something rooted in the New Testament.

Much that we have said about Jesus' personal body can be said, with appropriate adjustments, of His corporate body. Through the church, Jesus has contact with His people and the world. Through the members of His body, He speaks and is heard. Through the members of His body, His judgments are executed. When Jesus ascended into heaven, He sent His Spirit on the church at Pentecost.

Immediately, those poor slacker-disciples were transformed. Vacillating Peter became a bold preacher (Acts 2). No amount of intimidation could stop him. Peter and John healed a lame man, and Peter healed people with his passing shadow (Acts 3). Stephen, filled with the Spirit, looks like a second Jesus (Acts 6). And the whole story line of the apostles' lives begins to follow the life of Jesus (cf. Acts 12; the trials of Paul, etc.). As the patriarchs of a new Israel, the foundation stones of a new city, the apostolic members of the body of Christ, the apostles continue the ministry of Jesus, doing greater things than Jesus Himself had done. Wherever Jesus was, there was joy, life, power. Wherever the apostles are, that same joy and life and power is present, because they are leading organs of the corporate body.

Throughout her history, the church continues to be the place where Christ reaches out to the world, the site of His active presence. The church is not a continuation of the incarnation, nor a hypostatic union of divine and human. The church, joined to the God man, is a new humanity filled with the Spirit of Jesus, and as such is the body of Christ. Wherever she goes, there is the power and love and life and joy that was manifested in the personal body of the Word of Life. The church, H. Schlier says, is "the mode of the head's appearance in the cosmos." The personal body was the once-for-all and unique manifestation of God in the world; the corporate body, gathered to celebrate a meal on the Eucharistic body, is the continuing manifestation of God in the world. No man has seen God at any time, John writes. But the love that is God is visible in the church (1 Jn. 4:12).

The union-in-distinction of the personal and corporate body of Jesus is pithily expressed in Paul's claim that the church is "the fullness of Him who fills all in all" (Eph. 1:23). Calvin's comment on this verse is as striking as it is profound: "This is the highest honour of the Church, that, until He is united to us, the Son of God reckons himself in some measure imperfect. What consolation is it for us to learn that, not until we are along with him, does he possess all his parts, or wish to be regarded as complete!" This is why, Calvin adds, "when the apostle discusses largely the metaphor of a human body, he includes under the single name of Christ the whole Church." Christ is no more separable from His corporate body than He is from His personal body. He is perfected only when to His personal body is added His corporate. Jesus will not be content until He consummates His marriage to His bride.

Paul makes the move from personal to corporate body in the midst of his instructions on marriage in Ephesians 5, which include a reference to the body of which we are members (v. 30). In this chapter, however, the body language is set uniquely in the context of bridal imagery. The unity of a man and his wife constitutes them as "one flesh" (v. 31); they are two people united in a single life. Because of this, a man's care for his wife is an extension of his care for his own person, his own body: "husbands ought to love their own wives as their own bodies." Normally, one does not forget to nourish his own flesh, and his wife, now one-flesh with him, is to be nourished and cherished in the same way. If my wife gets cancer, I can't surgically remove her from me. I suffer the cancer along with her.

Paul applies this directly to Jesus. Genesis's declaration about the one-fleshness of man and wife is a statement about Christ and His church. Jesus is like the husband who cares for his own personal body, but Jesus is joined as one body with His bride, and He no more hates this bridal body than He can hate His own flesh. Paul states this directly: A man "nourishes and cherishes" his own flesh, and thus his bride, and this is analogous to Christ's nurturing of the church. Christ nourishes and cherishes her "because we are members of His body" (vv. 30–31).

Is Ephesians 5 talking about the visible, historical church or the invisible church of the elect? Which is so much united to Christ that it can be described as being "one flesh" with Him? Which is so much His body that He nourishes and cherishes it as He does His own flesh? Is the visible church the bride of Christ, or only the invisible?

The Reformed tradition is divided on this point. Some sectors of the Reformed confessional tradition have been as hesitant to apply bridal language to the visible church as to apply body language. In the Westminster Confession, only the invisible church is the "spouse" of Jesus Christ (25.1). Other Reformed Confessions, however, describe the visible church as "spouse" and "body." The Second Helvetic Confession (1566) reviews the history of the "church militant upon earth" (17.4) and then goes on to describe "this holy church of God" as the "spouse" and "beloved" of Christ (citing the Song of Songs 4:8 and 5:16), and concluding that this same church is "the body of Christ (Col. 1:24) because the faithful are the lively members of Christ, having Him for their head."

Reformed commentators, including Calvin, assume that Paul is speaking about the visible church in Ephesians 5, the church marked by the visible rite of baptism and the visible celebration of the Supper, both of which Calvin finds buried in Paul's description of marriage. The Westminster Confession, though, reserves the intimate language of bride and body to the "invisible" church and describes the "visible" church in political-familial terms. This makes things easy: One can be the subject of a "kingdom" without sharing in any intimate way with the King, and one can be a member of the visible kingdom of Christ without having any personal contact with Jesus.

Can we determine whether Paul is using the bridal language of Ephesians 5 to describe the "visible" or the invisible church? Here particularly it's important to recall what I noted above about the superiority of "historical/eschatological" to "visible/invisible." Operating with a visible/invisible model, we could read Ephesians 5 as a statement about the elect. Sure, Paul talks about a church that is still in need of cleansing, a church whose spots and wrinkles are still being removed. The "presentation" of the church "in all her glory" is still in the future (v. 27). But this could, on some readings, be interpreted as a passage that relates only to those elect, those invisible members of the visible church who will eventually be de-spotted and un-wrinkled. If we interpret the passage through the lenses of the historical/eschatological model, however, it's clear that Paul is talking about the church as she now is. This bride of Christ is not merely the church in her final state of glory, but the church in her process of glorification. The historical church, the visible church, is the bride of the Son and one flesh with Him, which Jesus treats as "His own body."

If this is true, then again we are left with some profound consequences for membership in the visible church. Baptism joins us to the church, and I have argued that the church is the body of Christ, not merely in some "honorary" or secondary sense, but in a real sense. Those who are baptized into the church share in Jesus Christ, and in Him they are introduced into the Triune fellowship of Father, Son, and Spirit. If the church is the body of Christ, the humanity of the Son of God, then this conclusion is inevitable. If the church, the historical and visible church, is the bride of Christ, then membership in the visible church involves us in marriage to Christ. We are members of His body as much as a bride is a part of her husband's flesh. Baptism is the wedding ceremony, and after the wedding we are promised that Jesus will treat us as His own body, for "we are members of His body" (v. 30).

Benefits of Membership

But what do we get when we get membership in the body of Christ? What are the benefits of membership in the historical church? The debate on this question often focuses on "soteriological" questions, and these soteriological questions are often questions linked to the elements of the *ordo salutis*. That is: Does baptism into the body of Christ in any sense justify the person baptized? Are baptized people adopted by God? Does baptism initiate sanctification? Is it linked with regeneration or glorification?

I will address these questions below, but first it's important to note that for the New Testament, "soteriological" issues are broader than the *ordo salutis* suggests. For the *ordo salutis*, soteriology is concerned with our relationship with God and the change in status and nature that occurs when the Spirit works on a person. Salvation has to do with our relationship with God and with the consequent changes in our spiritual condition. I don't want to minimize or ignore the Bible's teaching on these subjects. Eternal life is fellowship with the Father and His Son Jesus (Jn. 17). This fellowship has transforming effects on every dimension of our lives as our souls are refreshed and made new by the Spirit.

At the same time, the Bible does associate many other dimensions of Christian living with incorporation into Christ and His saving work. To be saved is to be priests and kings to God, fulfilling our human offices in the Last Adam (Rev. 1:6; 5:10). To be saved is to be a participant in the global mission of the church (Mt. 28:18–20). To be saved is to be gifted to edify the church (1 Cor. 12). To be saved is to receive a new family identity, to become part of the family of God stretching back to Abraham (Gal. 3:27–29).

To be saved is to receive promises of a future. To be saved is to take a particular stance in the world and to be on Jesus' side in the great cosmic battle that is human history. Baptism incorporates the believer into all that. By baptism, we are made kings and priests commissioned to take the gospel to the nations, gifted to edify the church, ingrafted into the family of Abraham, given hope for a new future. Baptism is "saving" in all these senses.

Some would want to distinguish between "official" aspects of the church and salvation. One can be gifted, even specially gifted by the Spirit, to work in the church without participating in the *life* of the church, without being truly a member of the body, without sharing in fellowship with God. They want to distinguish these external connections with the church from internal union with Christ. As I have been arguing, while the Bible does distinguish between internal and external, it doesn't distinguish them in this particular way. I don't see how a relationship with God can ever be purely legal or purely external. Those who minister in the church have been caught up in the work of the Spirit of Jesus, the saving work of the Spirit of Jesus. They are participating in the salvation of the world. Some who do this might eventually fall by the wayside (see the next chapter), but while they are in the church they are sharing the life that is the church's salvation. When Korah rebelled, the earth opened up and swallowed him, but before that he was a Levite who enjoyed the blessing of salvation from Egypt, drank from the water, ministered before Yahweh, and participated in the life of the redeemed people of God.

Even if we limit ourselves to the soteriological features of the *ordo salutis*, we find that the New Testament connects baptism to all these realities. These benefits are given to the baptized who share in the life of the body of Christ. For instance, Paul links baptism to justification in Romans 6:1–7. Verse 7 says "he who has died is justified from sin." Paul uses "justify" here to refer to our deliverance from the power and mastery of sin, not only to describe a verdict of righteous.[10] This deliverance from sin (what I've called

---

10. See my *Deliverdict* (Canon Press, forthcoming).

a "deliverdict"—an effective, liberating verdict) happens to those who die, and in the context the "death" is effective by baptism into the death of Christ: "Do you not know that all of us who have been baptized into Christ Jesus have been baptized into His death?" (v. 3). Paul's thought is: We have died to sin by baptismal union with Christ's death; anyone who has died is delivered from sin. Baptismal death with Christ is the instrument for delivering the emancipating verdict of justification, which opens up the possibility of new life for the baptized. In baptism, God judges sin, declares the baptized righteous, and delivers the baptized from death into the new life of the Spirit-filled body of God's Son.

We have examined 1 Corinthians 6:11 above, but we can make a few additional comments here. I take the washing mentioned here as a baptismal reference, and the washing is linked directly to sanctification and justification in the name of Jesus and in the Spirit. Washing in the name is not explicitly identified as the means or instrument of justification and sanctification here, but the three items in Paul's list—washed, justified, sanctified—present a cluster of descriptions of believers. Those who are washed are rightly described as the sanctified and justified. It is interesting, especially against the background of the *ordo salutis*, that "sanctification" precedes "justification" here. In every Reformed version of the *ordo*, the relation is reversed. But sanctification here does not, as in the *ordo*, refer to a process of increasing holiness and righteousness. Rather, it refers to the status of being a "holy one," a saint, and this status is granted by inclusion in the company of saints, the body of Christ. When we are washed in baptism, we become saints in this sense, consecrated by the Spirit, with access to the holy place of the church and the holy food reserved for priests. Justification too is linked with washing here. Those who are washed are righteous—included among the company of the righteous, made righteous in Jesus the Righteous.

Further, Galatians 3 connects baptism with adoption, another element of the traditional *ordo salutis*. Those who are baptized into Christ are "clothed" with Christ (3:27). This clothing represents office and identity. We are what we wear, and investiture is the key rite that installs someone in an office. To be baptized is to be granted an official place in the body of Christ. As Paul goes on, he shifts the image to a family one. We are not only invested with Christ, anointed in the Anointed One, but also become Christ's property (v. 29) and members of the family of Abraham (v. 29). There is no distinction here between the church as family-of-Abraham and the church as family-of-God. To be baptized is to become a child in the household of the Father and a brother to Jesus Christ because to be baptized is to be inducted into the family of God, the body of Christ.

And Titus 3:5, I think a baptismal passage, speaks about baptism as the "washing of regeneration." This again uses a term found in all the Reformed *ordo salutis* models and connects it to baptism. How is baptism the washing of regeneration? The word regeneration is used only twice in the New Testament, and in the other use (Mt. 19:28) it refers to a cosmic transformation or a coming epoch of history—"in the regeneration." I take it to refer to the New Covenant order, the order of life in Christ, in which the apostles will sit on thrones judging the tribes of Israel. If this is also the meaning in Titus 3:5, then baptism initiates the baptized into the regeneration, into the renewed humanity and renewed cosmos that is the body of Christ.

Confusion reigns in this area, however, when we forget what I emphasized in chapter 1, namely, that God is Personal, and that His grace is His personal favor expressed in various gifts. Confusion reigns more when these various blessings are treated as separate items on a list (something the *ordo salutis* itself tempts us to do). God is indivisible; Christ is not divided. Therefore, having Christ means simply having *Him*, and having Christ means having *God*. The various elements of the *ordo salutis* describe various facets of our personal union with our personal Lord Jesus. Too often, Protestants treat Christ's righteousness as some *thing* that can be shuffled around from person to person. Righteousness is not a thing or substance that is poured out or transferred. "Righteous" describes an inherent quality of Jesus and a verdict delivered by the Father in the resurrection, and this quality and this verdict become ours as we are united to Christ by the Spirit.

Thus, when asked, Do the baptized receive all the benefits of Christ, save persevering faith? I object to the form of the question. The baptized are implanted into Christ's body, and in Him share in all that He has to give. What baptism gives is not some collection of blessings, but the meta-gift of Christ, union with the whole Christ, head and body—necessarily head and body, for Christ is not divided. Membership in Christ's body doesn't exist without a connection to the head; no connection to the head exists without union with the body.[11]

In the Saved Society

This understanding of baptismal efficacy highlights the sociological dimension of baptism so long as we recognize that this "sociology" is not in conflict with the "soteriological" dimensions but co-involved with it. To be justified, on this view, is to share in the life of the justified community, the people whom God regards, because they are in Christ, as "righteous" in His sight. To be a saint is, in this view, to share in the life of the communion of saints. To be adopted is to be among the sons and daughters of the Father, and to be regenerated is to share in the life-in-the-Spirit that simply is the life of the body of Christ. Baptism delivers from one "culture," the culture of Adam, into a new "culture," the culture of the Last Adam. Baptism strips off the culture of flesh and inducts us into the culture of the Spirit.

This, it seems to me, is quite overt in some of Paul's writings. Romans 6 comes immediately after Romans 5, which describes sin and death's dominion over those who are in the first Adam. The condition of the unsaved is a participation in the first man and

---

11. One can, of course, imagine marginal cases. A man shipwrecked on a desert island is converted by a radio transmission and later dies without being rescued. He was never baptized, and he never was a member of a visible community, and yet he will be saved in the end. This kind of extreme case serves to qualify our ecclesiology and sacramental theology, but exceptions should not be central to either. Plus, the man in this hypothetical is in fact eventually united to the body of believers in the eschaton.

a participation in the world, the social and political and cultural order that is the product of Adam's sin. Paul then says that those who are baptized are delivered from this "Egypt" of Adamic life into newness of life, where they are to offer the members of their bodies as living sacrifices, as instruments of righteousness to God. Through baptism, they are delivered from the spiritual powers that reign over the world into the body of Christ, where the Spirit governs. Through baptism, they are delivered from the perverted influences and incentives that govern the world, the rivalries and mimetic envies that dominate it.

As argued in the previous chapter, Colossians 2 makes much the same point, showing that through our baptismal participation in the circumcision of Christ, we are delivered from the principalities and powers that dominate the world. We are under a new Lord and have no obligations to the demonic powers that once ruled us. We submit to Lord Caesar, but only because our ultimate loyalty is to the Lord Jesus. Flesh in all its dimensions is stripped off and we enter a new race by the Spirit.

Imagine when a Muslim converts. He comes to baptism with all sorts of familial and religious loyalties. He has lived in a twisted socio-religious world throughout his life, and this has patterned him with certain habits of conduct and grooved his mind in certain channels of belief and thought. The Spirit works on him to break through those grooves and to begin regrooving his mind and heart, and the Spirit also empowers him to break through the behavioral habits that have dominated his life and to resist the demonic encouragements that may well go with those habits. But the Spirit does all this through means. The Word is one means; the Spirit re-tools his heart and mind through the Scriptures and preaching. Baptism is another of these tools. Baptism drowns his old loyalties, and as he lives out his baptism, the Spirit progressively kills his old self and renews his loyalties, his commitments, his desires. Remembering his baptism, he remembers that he belongs to Jesus, not to Allah; he remembers that he is called to righteousness, not to sin. The Spirit uses that reminder in his maturation. Baptism also engrafts him into the fellowship of the church, where, led by the Spirit, believers live in humility, gentleness, joy, patience, love. Through the Spirit's power, he begins to catch the feel of living as a member of the baptized body, begins to breathe the air of joyful liberty and forgiveness, begins to imitate the gentleness and humility of his brothers and sisters. Baptism is one of the means the Spirit uses to regenerate him, to renew him in the image of God.

This particular way of stating the benefits of baptism assumes, of course, what I've said earlier in this book about the nature of human existence. If we are hard atoms of human stuff, then changing the network of relations in which we live has little effect on us. We still are what we are what we are. But if we are open-ended beings, incomplete in ourselves and complete only in fellowship with others (and ultimately Others), then changing our network of connections and becoming part of a new network is a radical change in identity, character, person. If our being is communion, then extraction from one communion and insertion into another is a change in our being. It is a new birth.

This is not an "immanentizing" of baptism. It doesn't reduce baptism to a "merely social" event. Baptism is a work of the Father authorized by the Lord Jesus and in which the Spirit is active. Baptism is not a merely social event because there is no such thing as a "merely social" event. God is always involved in every act and movement of the creation, and the universe teems with other spiritual beings, beneficent and malevolent, that are also active. The world is not a "merely social" reality because it is dominated by principalities and powers and controlled by sin and death (which are nearly personified in some parts of Paul's letters). It takes a divine act—a series of divine acts—to extract someone from the world and then plant him in the body of Christ. Baptism is one of those divine acts.

Water and the Spirit

When Jesus met with Nicodemus by night, He told the Jewish teacher that he had to be "born again of water and Spirit" if he hoped to enter the kingdom of God (Jn. 3:5). By chapter 3, John has already recorded John the Baptist's baptisms with water, quoting John the Baptist's contrast of his own water baptism and the Christ's Spirit baptism (1:19–34). This is the background to Jesus' words to Nicodemus. Jesus comes baptizing with the Spirit, but He claims that the new birth doesn't come from the Spirit only, but from the combined work of water and Spirit. Elsewhere in John 3, we learn that those who come for water baptism come because they have received "from heaven" (3:26–27). And we learn from John 4:1–2 that Jesus personally makes disciples even though He doesn't baptize them Himself.

Putting all this together, John's gospel points to the following scenario: God draws people to baptism. Unless God is preveniently at work, they would not come for baptism at all. But that drawing is not the new birth. The new birth comes not merely by water, not merely by Spirit, but by water and Spirit. And this is the way that Jesus makes disciples. He personally enlists disciples into His service through the physico-spiritual combination of water and the Spirit.

That's the way He made disciples in His own ministry. That's the way He still makes them.

4

Apostasy Happens

In the last two chapters, I have offered a very strong view of the efficacy of baptism. I've argued that the New Testament is talking about water baptism in most of the cases where it uses the word "baptism," and that it attributes virtually unbelievable powers to baptism. These wonders of baptism all arise from the fundamental fact that baptism initiates the baptized into the visible or historical church, which I have argued is the body of the Son of God, the Bride of Christ, and (one might add), the temple of the Spirit. Baptism is the water-crossing between membership in Adam and membership in Christ. Baptism grants the baptized a share in the great circumcision that occurred on the Cross, stripping away fleshly loyalties and habits and making us members of a new community. Membership in the corporate body never occurs without a personal connection with the Lord of that body. You can't be part of the Bride without being married to the divine Husband. Coming into the body through baptism means entering into a personal relationship with the Triune God, a relationship in which we are favored, accepted, given access to the Father and the table of His Son.

All that troubles many, and one immediate question will be: Can all that be ours without us doing anything in response? Don't we have to do something in response? And the answer to that is, of course, yes. But what? Once baptized by water into the corporate body of the Son of God, once we are one-flesh in the Bride of Christ, what's the appropriate response?

The answer to that is the favorite word in the Protestant vocabulary: Faith. Everyone who is baptized—*every* one—is brought into the body of Christ, ordained to be a priest before God, married to Jesus, and brought into the family of the Father, into the circle of God's personal favor. Everyone who is baptized is shown favor simply by the fact of their being baptized, for being named with the Triune name and being planted in the body of Christ are undeserved favors. But that favor does not last, or it does not produce fruit, without faith. Only those who respond in faith fulfill their priestly role rightly, persevere in the marriage covenant with Christ, stay in the family, remain in the circle of God's favor. Faith is the proper response to the favor of being baptized, the proper response from first to last. It is only by faith that we remain in the body of Christ, and only by faith that the water of baptism poured out on the earth of our bodies will bear fruit.

What is faith? Unfortunately, faith is sometimes described in pious code words that have little connection with everyday life. That's not how the Bible describes faith. The Bible gives us a thick, concrete description of faith. Faith is exercised in the midst of life's trials, not as an escape from them. For Abraham (who is *the* man of faith), faith expresses itself as obedience when he leaves Ur to go to a land he has not known (Heb. 11:8–12). He trusts that Yahweh will not abandon or betray him, and so he goes without knowing where he is going. For Abraham, faith means believing that God will accomplish what He says He will accomplish—giving Abraham a great name, a land, and a seed like the stars and sand. Yahweh told Abraham his seed would come through Isaac. Believing this, and trusting God to triumph over death to keep His word, Abraham obediently readies to offer Isaac in sacrifice. Abraham's faith involves believing that God's word is reliable because God is reliable, but it also means *acting* on this confidence in God and His Word. God says: Go here, and I'll be with you; faithful Abraham goes. God says: Kill Isaac, and yet I'll bring a seed from Isaac; faithful Abraham sharpens his knife. God says: I will give you a land and a great seed; faithful Abraham reorganizes his entire life around these unfulfilled promises.

Faith is, as the Reformers insisted, trust. Faith is also entrust-ment. It means identifying ourselves with Jesus and His Kingdom against all assaults, criticisms, persecutions, and threats, trusting that God will, sooner or later, vindicate us. Faith expresses itself in a life of loving, worshiping, and following Jesus. Faith is allegiance to the Son, taking His side in the great war that is human history. Faith is keeping faith, being loyal to the troth that is plighted in our marriage to the Son. Faith means believing what God says. Those who have faith respond appropriately to all God says, joining in His joyous song, trembling at His threats, believing that His promises will come to pass, obeying His commands. Faith is a gift of God, and only those who have faith until the end will be saved. Only those who believe, who have faith, who keep faith will be married to the Son in eternity. The Christian life is faith from first to last.

But what of the others? What of those who are brought into the church, the body of Christ, married to the Son of God, and who then fall away? What can we say about them?

The first thing to say is that those who receive the favor of God and then toss it aside are in worse shape than when they started. Israel was enslaved in Egypt, but unfaithfulness after the Sinai cov-enant would bring unprecedented curses—the curses of Egypt—onto her (Deut. 28:15–68, esp. vv. 58–60). Jesus says that impeni-tent Jerusalem will be charged with "all the righteous blood shed on the earth, from the blood of righteous Abel to the blood of Zecha-riah the son of Berechiah, whom you murdered between the temple and the altar" (Mt. 23:35). In Revelation, John foresees the horrific end of the "great city" of Jerusalem, which is judged as Egypt, Baby-lon, Tyre, and other rebellious Gentile cities had been judged (Rev. 17–18). Peter puts the point succinctly. Those who have escaped the miasma of the world and then return to its vomit and mud are worse than before: "The last state has become worse for them than the first. For it would be better for them not to have known the way of righteousness, than having known it, to turn from the holy com-mandment delivered to them" (2 Pet. 2:20–22).

Baptism is a covenant sign, and this brings blessing but also threatens cursing. An idolater who never knew Jesus will end up in hell. But someone who has entered into marriage covenant with Jesus by baptism and then turned to idols will suffer more severe wrath. To his idolatry, he adds the sin of adultery, unfaithfulness to the divine Husband. In this sense, baptism is always eternally effective. For those who believe, and persevere in believing, baptism is a witness of life unto life. For those who turn away, it is a witness of their broken faith, a witness of death unto death.

Apostasy Happens

The fact of apostasy is not in doubt. Anyone who has more than a couple of years' experience in the church has encountered apostasy. Someone hears the gospel, responds to it with apparent sincerity, joins the church, gets involved with all the ministries, starts teaching elementary-age Sunday School, gives up smoking and drinking, becomes diligent at work, takes care of his wife, and starts spending time with his kids. After a couple of years, he attends church less frequently and gives up his Sunday School class. You hear there are marital troubles, and before you know it, he's run off with his secretary and said he was never serious about Jesus anyway.

And experience is confirmed by multiple passages of the New Testament, that both warn about the possibility of apostasy and give examples of apostates. Jesus told an extended parable about apostasy, identifying the reasons why the seed of the Word dies before it brings a harvest (Mt. 13:1–9, 18–23). According to Paul, the Spirit "explicitly says that in later times some will fall away from the faith" (1 Tim. 4:1). This apostasy of the latter days is one of the sequence of events prior to the "coming of our Lord Jesus Christ, and our gathering to Him" (2 Thes. 2:1–3). This is not theoretical for Paul. He knows some who have "rejected and suffered shipwreck in regard to their faith," men such as Hymenaeus and Alexander, whom Paul himself "delivered over to Satan, so that they may be taught not to blaspheme" (1 Tim. 1:18–20).

The letter to the Hebrews is stuffed with warnings about apostasy. "Take care, brethren," the author writes, "lest there should be in any one of you an evil, unbelieving heart, in falling away from the living God" (3:12). Chapter 6 includes a chilling warning that "those who have once been enlightened and have tasted of the heavenly gift and have been made partakers of the Holy Spirit, and have tasted the good work of God and the powers of the age to come, and then have fallen away" cannot be "renewed again to repentance" (6:4–6). Those who have done so "again crucify to themselves the Son of God, and put Him to open shame" (6:6). And those who "go on sinning willfully after receiving the knowledge of the truth" face a "certain terrifying expectation of judgment," a fate more severe than the fate of those who sinned under the Mosaic covenant (10:26–31).

Peter describes people who have "escaped the defilements of the world by the knowledge of the Lord and Savior Jesus Christ," but then get "entangled in them." Their "last state" is worse than the "first," their ending so horrific that "it would be better for them not to have known the way of righteousness." Peter compares apostates to dogs who return to vomit and pigs who wash and then return to the mud (2 Pet. 2:10–22). Peter's entire epistle is a heads-up to his readers, a warning to help them to anticipate the challenges that lie ahead so they won't "fall from your own steadfastness" (3:17).

This is not a new theme in the New Testament. On the contrary, the entire Old Testament is a story of apostasy. Adam was, in a sense, the first apostate, turning from a condition of blessing to grasp at forbidden fruit. We may well hope that Adam did not remain apostate forever, but will be found in God's Paradise as he is in Dante's. Yet, he sinned and lost a status, blessings, and privileges he once had. He was cast out of the garden and lost access to the tree of life. Much of the story of the Old Testament is about Israel's multiple apostasies and Yahweh's refusal to let Israel withdraw from Him forever. Delivered from Egypt, given the blessing of land and the presence of Yahweh, nurtured and protected by her Lord and Father, Israel turned from Yahweh, worshiped false gods for much of her history and lusted after Gentiles and their gods. Yet, in the end, we are assured that "all Israel shall be saved." Throughout the Old Testament, Israel is on the verge of apostasy, called back in the nick of time by the Lord's intervention.

But there are examples in the Bible of some who fell away and did not return. Many of the redeemed from Egypt, though baptized in the sea and fed on Christ, died in the wilderness (1 Cor. 10:1–4). The Pentateuch names names: Korah, Dathan, and Abiram, for starters (Num. 16). After the conquest of Jericho, Achan, an Adam, grabbed some of Yahweh's loot and ended up under a pile of rocks (Josh. 7). King after king during the monarchy worshiped false gods and promoted the worship of false gods. We may have hope for Adam, but we hardly expect to meet Ahab when we enter the celestial city. Judas listened to Jesus, spoke to Jesus, ate meals with Jesus, ministered in Jesus' name, but eventually he sold it all off for thirty pieces of silver. Not all who are in Israel remain there. Not all Israel are of Israel.

No evangelical Christian disputes the facts and figures. As soon as we try to penetrate past the bare fact of apostasy, however, we discover intense, not to say vicious, conflict. What do we say about reprobates between baptism and apostasy? Did they ever believe? Were they ever joined to Christ? Did they ever enjoy the favor of God? Few Reformed people would deny that baptism as a covenant sign is double, offering blessing but potentially intensifying curses. But Reformed people differ in the way they describe the experience and status of a baptized reprobate before his apostasy. What do we lose if we leave?

Falling Away

According to many Reformed theologians, the answer seems to be "Not much." Apostasy happens in the sense that some leave the visible church, that external crust in which the real church is nestled, but those who leave never tasted of the kernel anyway. Since membership in the visible church is legal and political and external, rather than personal and intimate, their breach with the church is not a breach with Christ. You can't lose what you never had.

Calvin sets the terms for the Reformed treatment of this question in his comments on Hebrews 6:5. He asks how Hebrews 6 is consistent with the assurance that we are led by the Spirit in Romans 8. His answer is that "God indeed favours none but the elect alone with the Spirit of regeneration, and that by this they are distinguished from the reprobate; for they are renewed after his image and receive the earnest of the Spirit in hope of the future inheritance." Yet, he admits that "the reprobate also [have] some taste of his grace." God might well "irradiate their minds with some sparks of his light" and "give them some perception of his goodness, and in some sort engrave his word on their hearts." This explains the references to temporary faith in the parable of the sower. These warnings thus keep us "in fear and humility," guarding against the common human inclination to "security and foolish confidence."'

Along similar lines, Louis Berkhof claims that the Scriptural cases of apostasy "do not prove the contention that real believers, in possession of true saving faith, can fall from grace, unless it be shown first that the persons indicated in these passages had true faith in Christ, and not a mere temporal faith, which is not rooted in regeneration." There are some who "profess the true faith" but "are not of the faith," and apparently never were.

Robert Reymond takes a similar approach. He argues that "they teach that there is such a thing as 'temporary faith' which is not true faith in Christ at all," citing the Westminster Confession's statement about "common operations of the Spirit" for support (10.4). Reymond follows the Confession in insisting that those who fall away "never truly come unto Christ, and therefore cannot be saved." After a lengthy quotation from John Murray, Reymond concludes, "It needs to be stressed that those persons who have only this temporary faith were never God's elect and were never regenerated, and therefore are not true believers," a fact evidenced by their falling away.

That Murray quotation merits more than a moment's notice. Murray emphasizes "the lengths and heights to which a temporary faith may carry those who have it," and quotes Hebrews 6 and 2 Peter 2 in support. Scripture, he concludes,

> leads us to the conclusion that it is possible to have a very up-lifting, ennobling, reforming, and exhilarating experience of the power and truth of the gospel, to come into such close contact

with the supernatural forces which are operative in God's kingdom of grace that these forces produce effects in us which to human observation are hardly distinguishable from those produced by God's regenerating and sanctifying grace and yet not be partakers of Christ and heirs of eternal life.

While Murray's conclusion matches Reymond's—apostates were never partakers of Christ—Murray is much more expansive on the power and experience of temporary faith.

All this seems very workable. It provides a way of handling the apostasy passages while also affirming the perseverance of the elect. The only problem with this solution is that it doesn't reflect what the Bible usually says about apostasy and what the apostate has and enjoys prior to his apostasy. First John 2:19 perhaps speaks this way about apostates: "They went out from us because they were not of us." But many other passages indicate that people who eventually fall away received many benefits and blessings and had a personal connection with the Son and Spirit of the Father. Murray is right (even if, as I think, he doesn't go quite far enough): "It is possible to have a very uplifting, ennobling, reforming, exhilarating experience of the power and truth of the gospel" and yet lose it.

What do apostates possess before they go and fall away?

+ Some receive the word with joy, and experience life and growth for a time, Matthew 13:5, 20–21.
+ They are branches in the Vine, Jesus, John 15:2, 6.
+ They pass through the sea of baptism, 1 Corinthians 10:1.
+ They are baptized into the greater Moses, 1 Corinthians 10:2.
+ They eat spiritual food and drink spiritual drink, 1 Corinthians 10:4.
+ They drink of Christ, 1 Corinthians 10:4.
+ They have been enlightened, Hebrews 6:4.
+ They taste the heavenly gift, the word of God, and the powers of the future age, Hebrews 6:4–5.
+ They are partakers of the Spirit, Hebrews 6:4.

+ They receive heavenly blessing, like rain, Hebrews 6:7.
+ They are sanctified by the blood of the covenant, Hebrews 10:29.
+ They escape the defilements of the world, 2 Peter 2:20.
+ They know the Lord and Savior Jesus, 2 Peter 2:20.
+ They know the way of righteousness, 2 Peter 2:21.

In all these passages, the people described in these terms turn from Christ. Some seed falls on rocky ground and springs up quickly, but because of shallow roots and the choking effects of persecution, their life withers and dies (Mt. 13:20–21). Some enter the sphere of the new age, share in the body of Christ, share (*metoxous*) in the Spirit, taste the good things of the age to come, and confess Jesus as Lord, only to fall away (Heb. 6:4–6). Some branches are in the vine for a time, but because they don't bear fruit they are cut off and burned (Jn. 15:6). Some, Peter says, escape the world, know the Savior, come to know the way of righteousness, and then return to the world they had left (2 Pet. 2:20–22). Many who are baptized, who eat and drink from the Rock that is Christ, fall in the wilderness (1 Cor. 10:1–13).

Yet, all of these passages describe a real, although temporary, experience of favor, fellowship, and knowledge of God. These reprobates really were joined to Christ, really were enlightened and fed, really shared in the Spirit, and yet they did not persevere and lost what they had been given. Ultimately, these blessings and gifts are no help. Like the exorcized man who is infested with seven demons, their last state, Peter says, is worse than the first (2 Pet. 2:20). But the New Testament says pretty plainly that they have lost something real, which includes a relationship with the Spirit, union with Christ, and knowledge of the Savior.

Varieties of Apostasy

One of the problems with discussions of apostasy is we want to squeeze every apostate into the same mold. To listen to some, it appears that everyone who is baptized into the church, and then falls away at some later point, must have been a hardened hypocrite from beginning to end. A reprobate is always a reprobate and never experiences anything of the reality of God's favor, His acceptance, His blessings. This is far too one-dimensional to describe the infinite variety of human relationships to God. Each of us has a unique relationship to God. There are as many stories of losing faith as there are stories of gaining faith. There are as many varieties and types of unfaith as there are varieties and types of faith.

It's easy enough, of course, to imagine a melodramatic apostasy. The villainous reprobate knowingly joins the church just so he can disrupt it, all the while twirling his waxed moustache and rubbing his hands in fiendish glee. A secret service agent during the late 70s might, for instance, infiltrate a Catholic parish in Poland, hoping to discover Solidarity sympathizers in order to expose them and undermine their efforts. Well-studied, he pretends to go through a conversion, receives Catholic baptism, attends Mass regularly, and becomes involved in the parish. What do we say about this man? Certainly, we can say that he is reprobate, that his heart is not renewed, that he never enjoys the new birth. He enters the church under false pretenses and continues under false pretenses; he enters the church an unbeliever and remains so until the very end. God regards him as an enemy from beginning to end.

Even here, it's incomplete to say he is nothing but a reprobate, or that his relationship with the church or with Jesus is only "external." Every week at Mass, he hears Jesus speaking to him in the word. Every week, he shares a meal with Jesus and Jesus' family. He makes friends with believers from whom rivers of living Spirit flow. He might even participate in the ministries of the church in an effort to maintain his cover and delve deeper into the subgroup of Solidarity sympathizers. And in participating in the church's ministry, he might even be an unwilling and unwitting agent for the salvation of the world. All the time, he has received countless gifts from Jesus, the Lord of His church: He has received the gift of baptism, the gift of bread and wine, the gift of contact with the Spirit through Spirit-filled people, the gift of acceptance, for a time, in the body of Christ, and perhaps the gift of participation in God's saving action in history. He abuses and wastes these gifts; he hates and offends his Master at every turn; and all this will eventually increase the temperature of the hellfire that will swallow him. Yet the gifts were given. The cad who marries a woman for her money still marries her. His hypocrisy is not an automatic annulment. Our spy is a false member of the bride, but a part of the bride nonetheless.

Most stories of apostasy, I suspect, are not so straightforward as this. Most, I suspect, are more tragic than melodramatic, more *Othello* or *King Lear* than *The Perils of Pauline*.

Think of Saul.[12] First Samuel makes it clear that the gift of the Spirit affected Saul's heart. The Spirit was not only given for "official" business. As Saul left Samuel following his anointing, the Spirit came upon him (10:10) and "God changed his heart" (10:9). In the power of that Spirit, Saul hated and fought against the Ammonites who attacked Jabesh-gilead (11:6–11), and Saul displayed the fruit of the Spirit in dealing mercifully with those who had opposed his coronation (11:12–13). Yet, Saul sinned, then shifted blame or defended himself when Samuel confronted him (13:8–14; 15:17–31), and so the kingdom was removed from him. More personally, the Spirit, grieved at Saul's hardness (15:11), abandoned him and was replaced by an "evil spirit from Yahweh" that "terrorized him" (16:14). Saul did not persevere. He refused to listen to the voice of the Lord's prophet and eventually dined at the table of demons in the house of the witch of Endor. From the evidence of Scripture we are led to surmise that Saul was not eternally elect, but that is not our business. The Scripture says the Spirit "changed his heart" but later says Saul's heart turned from Yahweh. The Scripture says he received the Spirit, and then lost the Spirit.

In 1 Samuel, there is a parallel between the Spirit's presence in the tabernacle and His presence in the king. In chapters 1–4, we have an account of the perversity of the priests and the consequent capture of the ark, a story summarized by Phinehas's wife as a story of "Ichabod," the departure of the glory-Spirit from Israel. In chapters 10–15, we have the same story at an individual level:

---

12. The substance of these paragraphs was published as "Baptism and the Spirit," *Biblical Horizons* 85 (1996), available at:
www.biblicalhorizons.com/biblical-horizons/no-85-baptism-and-the-spirit

The Spirit comes to dwell with Saul but Saul's sins drive the Spirit out and Saul too becomes Ichabod, slain on the slopes of Gilboa. The parallel between the glory's presence among the people in His house and the Spirit's presence with the individual, Saul, works out the symbolism of the tabernacle. Since the Lord's house is an architectural image of the person, the pattern of the Spirit's presence in the tabernacle and temple manifests the pattern of His presence in and with persons. As the Spirit departed from Saul, so the Spirit departed from His dwelling place among the people, leaving the house desolate. Similarly, in Ezekiel 11:22–25 the cloud abandons the defiled temple, but it moves east to accompany the faithful remnant into exile.

One might argue that since Saul lived under the Old Testament, his experience does not speak directly to our situation. Saul, it might be argued, had the Spirit temporarily and officially, while the Spirit is now always given permanently and personally. But the situation envisioned in Hebrews 6:4–6 appears to be precisely that of Saul: Someone who received the Spirit falls away. To say that Saul's story is irrelevant also makes nonsense of Paul's admonitions to avoid "grieving" (Eph. 4:30) or "quenching" (1 Thes. 5:19) the Spirit. Paul's phrase echoes Isaiah 63:10: "they rebelled and grieved His Holy Spirit." According to Isaiah, grieved Yahweh "turned Himself to become their enemy, he fought against them." Isaiah is referring to Israel's adolescent tantrums in the wilderness, which are also described as bringing "grief" to Yahweh in Psalm 78:40. Yahweh had delivered Israel from captivity, provided water in the wilderness, rained manna from heaven, led them by the cloudy pillar of His Spirit, and yet when they rebelled He turned to become their enemy. Paul implies that the same can happen to us: If we rebel and grieve the Spirit, then the Lord turns and becomes an enemy.

In Isaiah 63, the outcome is happy. When Yahweh confronts her as an enemy, Israel "remembered the days of old, of Moses" and begins to seek the Lord (vv. 11–14). For Israel as a whole, grieving the Spirit is not the final end. And it is certainly possible for us to grieve the Spirit by our sins, suffer the Lord's enmity for a time, and then be brought to our senses. It is also possible, as happened with Saul, for us to grieve the Spirit by our disloyalty so that He departs and sends an evil spirit in His place to terrorize us.

Whatever we conclude about Saul's final destiny, his story is not a melodrama. He was a good son and was made a new man by the Spirit. He fought the Lord's battles for a time, but then he sinned and refused to repent. In the crisis moments of his life, he did not respond to the prophet with sackcloth, as David later did when confronted by Nathan (2 Sam. 11–12). In his latter days, Saul fought *against* the Lord's anointed, even as he sporadically acknowledged David's eventual triumph (1 Sam. 24, 26). Saul's is a tragic story of renewal and success that collapses into apostasy and pathetic failure, a story worthy of Sophocles or Shakespeare.

Or, think of Judas. Ultimately, as Jesus Himself said, Judas was a "son of perdition" (Jn. 17:12). He was reprobate, described as a "traitor" as soon as he is introduced in the gospel story (cf. Mt. 10:4) and as "a devil" (Jn. 6:70).

Yet, Judas accepted the call of Christ to be a disciple. He participated in the ministry of the Twelve. Like the other disciples, he was given "authority over unclean spirits, to cast them out, and to heal every kind of disease and every kind of sickness" (Mt. 10:1, 4). He was appointed among the Twelve to be "with Him" and to "preach" and to "have authority to cast out the demons" (Mk. 3:13–15). When a town or house received Judas, they received Jesus (Mt. 10:40). He had the authority to pronounce "peace" to those who accepted him, and to shake the dust from his sandals in curse against those who rejected him (Mt. 10:13–15). Judas was among the disciples who distributed bread to five thousand and picked up twelve baskets of leftover fragments (Mk. 6:30–33; Lk. 9:10–17). He was among those whom Jesus promised would sit on twelve thrones judging the tribes of Israel (Mt. 19:28).

He was one of those whom Jesus "wanted," and therefore whom Jesus "called" (Mk. 3:13). This is the language of election: Judas was among those whom Jesus "willed" to be a disciple (Greek, *ethelen*). And it is the language of calling (*proskaleitai*). Luke uses the verb "choose" (6:13), the same verb John (15:16) and Paul (Eph. 1:4) use to describe the sovereign choice of election. Obviously, this is not talking about an eternal and permanent choice. We know the end of the story, and Judas does not end well. The choice is a calling to apostolic ministry. In that sense, though, Judas was "elected" and "called."

But Judas's was not merely an "external" and "official" call, since Mark says Judas was called according to the will of Jesus to be "with Him" (Mk. 3:14). Until he went to the priests to betray Jesus, he stood on Jesus' side in the various conflicts with Pharisees and scribes that wracked Jesus' ministry. Did Judas have a "personal relationship" with Jesus? Yes, of course, he did. He was "with Him" not only in proximity but in intimate personal relationship. Judas heard Jesus speak in public and heard His private explanations of parables (Mk. 4:10). Judas was one who was "given the mystery of the kingdom of God" (Mk. 4:11). He was an "insider" and not an "outsider" (Mk. 4:11), one of the few to whom Jesus revealed His coming suffering and death (Mk. 10:32–34). Judas ate with Jesus (Mt. 26:20) and traveled with Jesus. He was among those for whom Peter spoke when he said, "we have believed and have come to know that You are the Holy One of God" (Jn. 6:69). Even when he came to Jesus in Gethsemane, Jesus greeted him as "friend" (Mt. 26:50). He wasn't kidding: Judas had been a chosen friend, a fact that made the pain of betrayal all the more agonizing.

We simplify things unnecessarily and illegitimately if we say that Judas' relationship with Jesus was purely "external." How can two people talk to one another and remain entirely "external" to one another? Speech breaks through the barriers that separate man from man, and all speech is, as Augustine said, an outpouring of one soul into another. Jesus got on the inside of Judas, of that we may be certain. How can two people share a meal and remain entirely external to one another? They eat from the same loaf, share the same roast; the molecules of the one food are shared by two. No, we oversimplify if we say Judas is merely a reprobate. Jesus put the two sides of Judas' career together when he said, "Did I Myself not choose you, the twelve, and yet one of you is a devil?" (Jn. 6:70).

Judas's story is as tragic and paradoxical as Saul's. He is the chosen devil, the elect betrayer, the called traitor.

Election, Time, and Relation

What's at stake here is not, it must be emphasized, the doctrine of eternal election or the Reformed insistence that God not only elects but reprobates, all before the foundation of the world. I fully agree with the Reformed tradition on that point.

As I pointed out in chapter 1, the issues at stake are background issues concerning time and relation and how these affect the formulation of the doctrine of election. Let's start with time: Some Reformed theologians formulate the doctrine of election without due consideration to time. Election effectively means that God has ordained the end of every man's life, his final destiny. Of course, it is always said that God ordains the means as well as the ends, but this still doesn't give sufficient emphasis to the fact that what God ordains is the *whole life-story* of each and every human being, not merely the final act or the means of reaching that final act. This doesn't mean the final destiny is left in human hands. On the contrary, the ultimate destiny, not to mention the penultimate and the antepenultimate destiny, is decreed by God.

Once we recognize that God ordains *time* with all its changes, all its ups-and-downs, we can get a better grasp of how election fits with the various apostasy texts in the New Testament. Think of the parable of the sower, and particularly the seed that produced a temporary burst of life but then withered because it lacked rooting in the soil (Mt. 13:20–21). What did God ordain in that story line? The final end of death? You bet. How about the fact that the man heard the word? Yes. That he received it with joy? That too. That he had no roots? Yep. That he exercised faith for a time? Yes. That his faith was temporary? Of course. That affliction and persecution arose from the world? Yes. That he fell away? Of course. Every moment of the story, every stage of the development, was completely under the sovereign oversight and control of God. What God ordained was not just the end of apostasy, but the whole story of sowing-hearing-joy-unrootedness-affliction-and-apostasy.

Or think of Jesus' description of the vine and branches in John 15. Did God ordain that the branches be in the vine? Yes. Did He plan for them to be united to Jesus? Yes. Did He anticipate that some do not abide? That too. That the ones who fail to abide are unfruitful? Yes. That the unfruitful vines are finally cast out? Of course. From beginning to end, the whole story line of the unfruitful branches is ordained by God. Before the foundation of the world, He scripted the whole story of union-with-Christ-which-does-not-last.

The second key element of this is the fact that God is personal, or tri-personal to be precise. He relates to His creatures, and particularly to man, Personally. To be saved means to be in a relationship of trust, friendship, sharing, fellowship, love, and life with the Triune God. There is no such thing as an "impersonal" relationship with God. Even the enemies of God who never enter the body of Christ are in relation to Him, a relationship of enmity. Since this is so, we can't think of salvation or grace as a thing or object we possess. God is not an impersonal determining force, nor is salvation some kind of impersonal stuff handed over, spilled out, or poured into human beings. His grace *is* His favor, expressed in gifts. God's grace is His personal favor to sinners who don't deserve His favor in the least.

When we combine these two points—time and relation—we come to a better understanding of election and reprobation. God ordained an individual story line for each human being who exists or ever will exist. That story line is a story of God's relation to that human being, and because it is a story line in time, the relationship between God and the person changes and develops. Saved people are not in a static-state relationship with God; they are always either moving closer or further away, usually both simultaneously but in different respects. God's relation to His eternally elect people is like a marriage, and like any marriage, it has moments of bliss and moments of tension and strife. Likewise, God's relation to the reprobate changes in time. For a time, a reprobate might come into His favor and respond with faith. Later, they will fall away, cease abiding, and fall out of His favor.

Ahh, you say, but the change is all from one side. It's only our changes that create tension or bliss, for God remains unchangeably the same. But if this is true, then when we try to put election in this relational setting, we lose election, because we leave our final destiny in our rather unsteady hands. As we saw in chapter 1, the premise of that objection is not true. God is not bound by time. He created time, oversees time, controls it, and enfolds it as Alpha and Omega. Yet, He is immanent in time, moves by the rhythms of the creation He has made, and responds to human beings in time. In one sense, conversion or apostasy is entirely a change in man; God has plotted it all from the beginning, and his change of course doesn't change God's course. In another sense, however, God changes His view of and attitude toward the convert and the apostate, moving in one case from wrath to favor and in the other from favor to wrath.

It is this latter sense that is most relevant for understanding baptism, membership in the body of Christ, and apostasy. This latter sense is, in fact, the relevant one for our experience. For, being historical creatures, we are bound by time. We encounter the God who is beyond time, but we don't encounter Him beyond time. We encounter God as He works in time. And in time, we respond to Him and He responds to us.

The great prooftext demonstrating that election and reprobation are not in the least incompatible with a strong understanding of apostasy is Romans 9. That is the great reprobation text in the New Testament, teaching as it does that God has mercy and hardens as He pleases, in accord with His own perfect will. But the reason Paul brings up this point is to explain the apostasy of Israel. That is the anguishing fact that leads into a discussion of reprobation in the first place. Reprobation is the answer to the question, Why is Israel according to the flesh not responding to the gospel of her own Messiah? And part of Paul's answer is that they are not responding because God, the Potter, has made some vessels for destruction and some for salvation.[13]

---

13. I call this a "part" of Paul's answer because there are deep redemptive-historical things going on in Romans 9 as well.

Far from being incompatible with apostasy, reprobation is actually a *theory of apostasy*.

Assurance

Where does this leave us? Can we ever have any assurance that we are in Christ, *permanently* in Christ, in Christ's hand so that we cannot be snatched away? The view I've outlined so far suggests a negative answer. Baptism incorporates the baptized into the corporate body of the Son of God, where he is given a share in the abundant life of the church in communion with the Triune God. He is called to keep faith, yet I'm also telling him that some who are baptized into Christ's body, and live the life of that body, eventually fall away. How can he know he's not one of them?

Before taking that question head on, it's important to stress that the Bible teaches we *can* know we are His. The Bible in many ways promises us that God will retain those who are His own. Jesus assures His disciples that no one can snatch them from His hands (Jn. 10:26–30). Paul's letters breathe out a triumphant air: Nothing can separate us from the love of God in Christ Jesus, "neither death, nor life, nor angels, nor principalities, nor things present, nor things to come, nor powers, nor height, nor depth, nor any other created thing" (Rom. 8:37–38). The God who began a good work will, Paul says, bring it to complete maturity in the day of Jesus (Phil. 1:6).

But to whom are these promises addressed? How can I know they are addressed to *me*? Simple quotation of words of assurance from the New Testament does not solve the existential problem of assurance for an individual. Paul says, "Nothing shall separate *us* from the love of God in Christ Jesus," but how do I know that "us" includes "me"? Paul doesn't appear to tell me. He doesn't say, "Nothing shall separate Peter J. Leithart from the love of God in Christ Jesus." How can I know that I'm included in that "us"?

One way of addressing this question is to examine one's own life for fruits that will only be produced by the Spirit in a person who is eternally elect. Trying to pin down what those fruits are is very difficult. Joy is a fruit of the Spirit (Gal. 5:22), but the seed that falls on the rocky ground rejoices in the word for a time (Mt. 13:20).

How can I know that my joy is not going to go *poof* as soon as persecution begins? Love is a fruit of the Spirit as well, one that John says is the distinguishing mark of the one who is born of God and knows God (1 Jn. 4:7). Yet, when I measure my love for my brothers and sisters by the standard of 1 Corinthians 13, I wonder if I have any love at all. How much have I really sacrificed of my own convenience and projects for someone else? Not much. Peace is a fruit of the Spirit (Gal. 5:22), but how can I know the difference between presumptuous false peace of conscience and the peace that passes human understanding? How can I know whether I have peace because I have so seared over my conscience that nothing can touch it, or because Christ's blood has penetrated past the flesh to cleanse my conscience?

Perhaps we can try faith. Faith is a gift of God (Eph. 2:6), and it's by faith that we are joined forever in fellowship with Christ. Yet, the Reformed tradition teaches that some have temporary faith. The Canons of Dort reject those

> Who teach . . . [t]hat the faith of those who believe for a time does not differ from justifying and saving faith except only in duration. For Christ Himself, in Matthew 13:20, Luke 8:13, and in other places, evidently notes, beside this duration, a threefold difference between those who believe only for a time and true believers, when He declares that the former receive the seed on stony ground, but the latter in the good ground or heart; that the former are without root, but the latter have a firm root; that the former are without fruit, but that the latter bring forth their fruit in various measure, with constancy and steadfastness (Fifth Head, Paragraph 7).

Though the point of this passage is to emphasize the differences between true and temporary faith, the whole statement acknowledges the reality of temporary faith. So, how can I know that my faith is permanent? By looking at a typical Reformed answer to this question, we begin to see how assurance becomes a problem within Reformed theology.

According to one line of Reformed thinking, we can be assured we are justified forever because we can be assured that we have justifying faith. And we can know in part because true, justifying, saving faith is an entirely different—some say "qualitatively" different—kind of thing from temporary faith. Following the Canons of Dort, Turretin attempts to explain the differences between temporary and true, saving faith. Against the Remonstrants, he claims that temporary faith differs "in its entire species from the faith of true believers." Temporary faith differs from its genuine form as to "internal principle and manner of rooting." True faith comes from "the Spirit of regeneration," while temporary faith from "the Spirit of illumination." The mode of rooting differs because one is superficial while the other is deep. More fully, true faith is "deep, most internal, vital, friendly and efficacious," while temporary faith "sticks to the uppermost surface of the soul (to wit, in the intellect); it does not penetrate to the heart, nor does it have true trust in Christ." Elsewhere, he says that temporary faith has only "superficial and theoretical" knowledge, and that its assent is "weak and slippery, connected with perpetual hesitation and wavering."

In some respects, Turretin is simply summarizing, as the Canons of Dort do, the implications of the parable of the sower. The seed that is not "deeply rooted" springs up but eventually withers. Yet, Turretin's discussion is problematic in a number of ways. Perhaps the oddest thing is the way Turretin encourages us to turn attention to the quality of faith. It is hard to see how a discussion like this can do anything but *undermine* assurance. Is my faith characterized by "panting for the grace of Christ from an intimate sense of [my] own misery and apprehending it with a firm faith (but with submissive humility)"? If I'm honest, I have to say, "Not always."

Does that mean my faith is temporary? Temporary faith resides in the "mouth" and never in the heart, and if it goes to the soul at all "it is rather in the intellect through knowledge than in the will through love." How am I to know the difference? How can I locate where faith lodged itself, in the will or in the intellect? Turretin admits that temporary faith might go to the heart, but it never gets the whole heart: "it never delivers itself wholly to God," never "gives itself absolutely and unlimitedly without any restriction." How can I read that without concluding that I've only got temporary faith? Is my faith firm, whole, absolute, unlimited, unreserved? All the time? Doesn't true faith waver? Don't *believers* pray, "Help my unbelief"?

Trying to solve the problem of assurance by examining the quality of faith, hope, and love invariably leads into an abyss. And the same thing can happen with some accounts of the "testimony of the Spirit." The Spirit's work is real, and it certainly produces confidence, but in the hands of some, the testimony of the Spirit is a purely private inner experience, with the Spirit whispering quietly to our spirit. But how can we distinguish the witness of the Spirit from the self-deception of our own hearts? How can we be sure that it's the Spirit witnessing to our spirit and not our own spirit bearing false witness to itself? How, in short, can we be assured that the inner assurance we experience is not self-deception? That line of thinking is self-defeating and abyssal. We will never get to the end of the string of questions if we only take into account the inner witness of the Spirit. Every whisper we hear inside could be either the Spirit or our spirit, and how can we ever tell?

The Spirit works through means and whispers His witness that we are the children of God through words, through signs, through other people, through things. How can I know that my name belongs within the "us" when Paul says "Nothing can separate *us* from the love of God which is in Christ Jesus"? How can I know that the Spirit is speaking to me?

Easy: I *heard* Him.

God addressed this promise to me in my baptism; He addresses this promise to me every week when I hear a minister pronounce the absolution of sins; He renews this promise to me, out loud, every time I hear a sermon; He addresses this promise to me every week when I come to His table to eat and drink in His presence. Through these the Spirit woos me, hugs me, encourages me, kisses me, feeds me, visits me, clothes me, challenges me, rebukes me, convicts me, changes me. There is no doubt that the Spirit is addressing *me*. I can hear Him speak, though He uses human vocal chords or ink and paper. I have no doubt that I'm included in the "us" that is not separated from Christ because I heard God include me in that "us."

When I hear the Spirit speak, I'm being called to believe Him. In baptism, He says, "I've washed you so you can be part of My family and come to My table and draw near in worship." Believing that, I live with confidence that I'm the son of a heavenly Father and draw near through Jesus to worship Him in the Spirit. Believing what God says in baptism, I consider myself dead to sin and strive to yield my members as instruments of righteousness. In absolution, God says, "Your sins are forgiven." I believe that, and when my conscience strikes me, I remind myself of what God said, the God who is greater than my heart. I remind myself of what I *heard* Him say. In a sermon, He says, "Look at what I've done. Trust me, and obey." I believe what He says in the sermon, and in faith I strive to obey Him. At the table, He says, "Here I offer you life through the Son." I believe, and come to the table expecting to be renewed. Jesus says, "Come over for dinner, and I'll feed Myself to you for your life." I trust Him, so I come to His table as often as I can, trusting that all my hungers will be satisfied as I feast with God's people on the bread of life.

Ahh, but someone sitting next to me has received the same baptism, hears the same words, eats at the same table, and yet falls away. He might even believe awhile, believe strongly, believe rejoicingly, and yet fall away. So, how do these words and hugs and kisses and feasts assure me of anything?

Ultimately, we cannot explain this. How can a creature who owes his very existence and every breath and every heartbeat to his Creator hate that Creator? How can a baptized church member who has been privileged to be adopted into *the* Royal Family turn from it? How can anyone who has been brought into the abundant life of the body of Christ find some other life appealing? How can anyone seek good by departing from the source of all good? Ultimately, we, with Paul, have to appeal to the fact of God's hardening. Why do some turn away, abandoned by the Spirit? Because God determines to turn away from them, and this fulfills His own mysterious, yet perfect, purposes.

There are unfathomable mysteries here, but in one sense the explanation is very simple. Someone who is grafted into the body of the Son of God and believes for a time, and then falls away, has simply failed to keep faith. He believed and then he stopped believing. For some it is slow. Some stop believing in a moment. For some, such as Herman Melville, the wrenching departure lasts a lifetime. Yet, fundamentally, the story is the same: Apostasy happens when a friend betrays his utterly faithful companion; when a woman leaves an utterly devoted husband; when a member of the body of the Son of God amputates himself; when a rebel grieves the Spirit and the Spirit departs; when a slob escapes the miasma but then decides he prefers the mud pit. Apostates may hear the promise, receive the kind gifts of God, and never believe. They may receive all these things and keep faith for a time. Ultimately, they fall away because they do not keep on believing. They do not keep faith.

Apostasy doesn't sneak up on people who are keeping faith. God is not in the business of cutting off sincere believers just for kicks. He is not the wanton boy who tortures flies for sport. He does not send faithful believers to hell at the last judgment. He is kind and good, and merciful to those who have even the smallest grain of faith. Those who enter the body of Christ in baptism, trust in and confess Jesus, seek Him in His Word and at His table, serve His people humbly, live in fellowship with brothers and sisters, seek to produce the obedience of faith—these have nothing to fear. They are included within the "us" that Paul says will never be separated from the love of God in Christ Jesus, and they are reassured of that every time they hear God address them in word, in water, and in bread and wine. If we are doing all the things that Jesus means by "abiding" in Him, we can be sure that we will be in the Vine to the end. Faithful believers will not discover on the day of judgment that they were reprobate after all. Happy marriages do not end in divorce. God doesn't spring divorce on a faithful bride.

This is not self-trust, since all these forms of "abiding" in Christ are gifts of God that are effective through the work of His Spirit. If we trusted ourselves, we wouldn't pay any attention to God's declaration that we are forgiven, because we wouldn't see ourselves as in need of forgiveness. Apart from faith, eating a morsel of bread and drinking a thimble of wine every week appears absurd. How can this table contribute in any way to the fulfillment of my ultimate destiny? To this question, faith is a child: My Father says it works, so I believe it works.

Perseverance is always perseverance, and maturation, in faith and trust. Perseverance is for that very reason also perseverance in *dis*trust of self. The New Testament shows that faith has fruits, and the Reformed tradition has insisted that the faith by which we are justified is never alone in the person justified. But we never come to the point where we mature from trust to works. Faith is nourished and nurtured; it grows stronger and more assured as we stick with Jesus. But it is faith from first to last.

And this is the pathway of assurance. Too often the Reformed tradition has degenerated into a morbid form of self-analysis that is actually much closer to medieval piety than to the first Reformers. We are trained to stand outside ourselves and adopt a stance of objectivity in order to examine our performance, the strength of our faith, the consistency of our obedience. If our life matches our profession, then we are assured of our standing in Christ. Then we "know that we know" (1 Jn. 2:3). This is not, I think, what the New Testament means when it talks about assurance. "Knowing that we know" means experiencing the assurance that we are in a relationship of love—a "knowing" relationship—with God in Christ through the Spirit. We come to this experience of assurance in the midst of our abiding in Christ, not by standing outside our relationship with Christ and evaluating it as outsiders. We come to that experience as we trustingly, believingly remember and improve our baptisms, hear the Word of our beloved Husband, and feast as His Bride at His table.

5

A Tale of Three Servants

Once there were three young men who served a great King. On the recommendation of the Crown Prince, each was brought to the palace, given a ritual bath, clothed in the garments of a page, and placed in the King's service.

The King accepted them warmly and treated them as if they were his own sons. When he met with them, he told them the history of the kingdom and, through authorized tutors, taught them the ways of the court. As he spoke, they not only learned how to behave as courtiers, but also grew to love and trust the wise king more and more. Often they served table at royal feasts, but occasionally the King would invite them to sit down and join the merriment. Life in court was abundant with joy and peace.

As the three young men grew in skill, they accompanied the King on military campaigns and diplomatic missions. Each fought bravely, and through their prowess and leadership the King came to rule a larger and larger territory. One of the young men became a herald. The King sent him on diplomatic missions and trusted him to negotiate with rulers in the surrounding countries. The three became very famous in the kingdom.

But the three were not all of one mind about the King and the privilege of being in his service. The first servant was, in fact, a spy for a neighboring kingdom. He entered the King's service in order to disrupt his court and undermine his plans for conquest. He listened to the King and, to maintain his cover, conformed his conduct to the King's desires. Inwardly he chafed when the King spoke.

Instead of growing in his love and devotion to the King, he found the King's words and habits increasingly irksome. For some years, the King suspected him of treachery and was cautious about sending him on royal missions. Yet the King continued to show him every kindness and treated him with such friendly warmth that no observer could have guessed the King's suspicions. Eventually, the servant was discovered sneaking out of the palace by night to send a report to his true master. Grieved and angry, the King ordered him to be imprisoned and later signed an execution order.

The second servant had come from a poor and insignificant family and was delighted to be a member of the court. He learned all he could about court life and fighting and looked forward with great eagerness to the times when the King would invite him to sit at his table to share a meal. He trusted and loved the King, and that love and trust seemed to be deepening with every passing month.

It did *not* last. The servant began to turn against the King when he accompanied the first, treacherous servant on a diplomatic mission. As they traveled, the first servant spoke about the King's conquests. First he only asked questions, but soon he made bold assertions about the King's cruelty. The second servant defended the justice of the King, but through a combination of lies, cleverly chosen omissions, and misleading innuendos, the treacherous servant was able to shake his friend's confidence.

As suspicions grew in the second servant, the King's words no longer sounded as innocent or wise as they had once, and the servant began to wonder what the King really wanted when he invited the servants to dine with him. He thought of talking with the King about the first servant's charges, but when the first servant was imprisoned, it seemed that all the suspicions had proven true and he was afraid to reveal himself. Late one night, he slipped out of the palace and ran away to a neighboring court, where he served for the rest of his life.

The third servant was at first the least promising of the three. He had no lack of natural skill and intelligence, but there was a belligerent streak that led to continuous strife with other courtiers, and often with the King himself. He was initially suspicious of the

King's favor, questioned the King's advice, and ate little when he sat with a surly frown at the King's table.

Yet, whenever he failed at some task, or was caught in some fight, or insulted the King, the King showed superhuman forbearance. He forgave him completely and continued to teach and talk to him. During the second year of his service, the servant's heart began to melt and he began to delight in the King's company, his words, and his table. He learned to show the same patience and kindness toward his fellow courtiers that the King had shown him. He served the King loyally for many decades, became a great man at court, and fought and won many battles for the King, including one against an opposing army led by the fallen second servant who had left the court. When he became an old man, he taught the younger courtiers the ways of the court. He had a special gift for bringing unruly pages into line. When he died, full of years, he received a lavish state funeral and was greatly grieved and missed by the court.

Shortly before he died, the third servant lay on his bed. The spring sun shone through the great window of his room in the palace. His grandson, now a page to the very same, ageless King, was sitting beside him. His mind wandered, as old men's minds do, to his youth, and to the two pages who had begun their service with him.

"But the first servant was *never* a servant of the King," his grandson was saying.

"Yes, that is true. He was a traitor from the beginning," the old man replied. "And yet, as soon as he was dressed in the very garments you now wear, he was a King's servant. In spite of himself, he even did the King good service."

"But he didn't really know the King."

"Not as he should have, certainly. But the King shared with him as lavishly as he shared with the rest of us. He sat at the King's table, learned from the King, wore the King's livery, carried the King's banners. He lived as abundantly as we all did. All the while there was treachery in his heart. Yet I am sure there were times when his heart bent to the king and he recognized his treachery as the evil it was. I can remember times when there was a gleam of a tear in his eye, and times when he laughed, heartily and sincerely I think, at the King's stories. He would have had to be inhumanly hard not to melt a little before the King's warmth."

"And the second servant was just like the first. He too turned traitor."

"Oh, no, no, no. His story is quite different. The end is the same, surely, but the path toward that end is another story altogether. You see, he loved the King and trusted him. He loved the King better than I."

"At the beginning . . ."

"Yes, at the beginning. If the King had passed judgment during that first year, I am sure I would have been cast out of the palace and the second servant would have been honored above all the servants of the house. I am happy the King does not pass judgment so quickly. I made myself such an annoyance. I still feel pain at the memory, though the King seems to have forgotten it completely."

"But how could that servant turn so completely? Surely he knew nothing of the King's spirit."

The old man smiled. "You are very young. Everything looks very plain, very neat and clean, to a young man. But it was not neat and clean. The second servant knew the King's spirit. He tasted the King's spirit, and that spirit inspired him to great things, great things *for the King*. But then he forgot. He pushed down the King's spirit. Something happened deep in his soul, and somehow he forgot all the kindness, all the laughter, all the words, all the feasts. He began to suspect the King's kindness. He began to think the King was laying traps for him, and so he foolishly thought he would lay a trap for the King."

The bright afternoon deepened to crimson. Neither the old man nor his grandson spoke for a long time. Evening sounds and the aroma of the early honeysuckle came through the window on the cooling air.

"How could they have done it?" the young man said at last. "They had everything they could have asked for, an abundant life in the service of the King. What were they looking for?"

Breathing heavily, his grandfather answered, "I do not know. It is a great mystery. And yet it happened."

The grandson shivered. "It is very frightening," he said quietly. "What is?"

"It is frightening to think that someone who received so much, someone who was so loyal, could turn so completely. I am afraid I might do the same."

The old man reached and touched his grandson's hand. "Do not fear. The King will keep you. Stay near him. Trust what he says. Do not be suspicious of him. Enjoy his feasts. Spend time with the other pages and the older courtiers. You wear the livery of a royal servant, and that is a sign of his favor. Keep faith with the King, and all will be well."

And it was.

Appendix: The Sociology of Infant Baptism[14]

Among modern Christians, including many who practice infant baptism, the Baptist position seems obvious and commonsensical while the paedobaptist position seems to run against the grain of human life. *Of course*, one enters a religious community only when he consents to it. It violates our sense of the voluntary character of religion and morality to suggest that infants can be introduced, without their consent, into a religious life. As a result, an ether of defensiveness and desperation hovers over some defenses of infant baptism.

In this paper I shall argue, somewhat implicitly, that the obviousness of the Baptist position depends upon assumptions about the nature of Christianity and the relationship of religious to "ordinary" life, especially the relationship of religious and cultural nurture (which is a specific form of the "Christ and culture" question). Once these assumptions are challenged, and they *are* open to challenge, the illusion that the Baptist position is obvious begins to fade.[15] Positively and more explicitly, I shall be offering a

---

14. This paper was first published by James Jordan in *Christendom Esays: Biblical Horizons Issue No. 100.* I am grateful to Jim for publishing it, and for permission to include it here as an appendix.

15. This paper reflects the influence of several articles on baptism: Mark Searle, "Infant Baptism Reconsidered," in *Living Water, Sealing Spirit: Readings on Christian Initiation,* ed. Maxwell E. Johnson (Collegeville: Liturgical Press, 1995), 365–409; Andrew D. Thompson, "Infant Baptism in the Light of

meditation on the view of human life and society implied by infant baptism and a defense of that view.

As an entry into the discussion, we can consider the differences between Baptist and paedobaptist views of Christian nurture of children. The motivation and initial situation are the same for both. Christian parents hope and pray their children will become mature believers. Equally obviously, infants do not come into the world reflecting the character of Christ. It is not right to say they are completely unformed, for they are born in the form of the first Adam. Thus, what all Christian parents desire is that their children die to the form of Adam and come to new life according to the pattern of Christ.

Ultimately, this formation occurs by the power of the Spirit. God re-shapes us as the potter does the clay; no one constructs Christlike character by his own efforts, nor does any other human being do it for us. At the same time, Scripture makes clear that, to use the language of the *Westminster Confession of Faith*, secondary means are real and have real efficacy. The Spirit forms and molds an infant into a mature Christian through created means, and baptism clearly has something to do with this. Jesus told His disciples they were to make disciples of the nations through baptism and teaching, and being a disciple means becoming like the Master (Mt. 10:24–25; 28:19–20). Thus, baptism is one of the means by which we become formed according to the image of Christ; it is one segment of the "tracks" that lead from the initial situation (image of Adam) to the goal (image of Christ).[16] So then: What

---

the Human Sciences," in *Alternative Futures for Worship: Volume 2: Baptism and Confirmation,* ed. Mark Searle (Collegeville: Liturgical Press, 1987), 55–102; Rowan Williams, "Sacraments of the New Society," in *Christ: The Sacramental Word,* eds. David Brown and Ann Loades (London: SPCK, 1996), 89–102; Vern S. Poythress, "Indifferentism and Rigorism in the Church: With Implications for Baptizing Small Children," *Westminster Theological Journal* 59 (1997):13–29.

16. In the back of my mind is John Milbank's emphasis on *poesis,* his claim that human being is creative being, sharing in the creative activity of God. One can even say that, in a certain sense, human beings create *ex nihilo,* causing new things and even entirely new categories of things, to come into existence—cakes

does *infant* baptism tell us about the "mechanisms" that the Spirit employs to remake us, translating us from the image of Adam to the image of Christ?

In general, we can answer this question as follows: The Baptist position implies that this reshaping begins "outside" ordinary means of nurture and development, and chronologically after this ordinary nurture has begun. Baptist parents do not consider their children to be fully Christian until they have reached a certain age and made a decision. The nurture of their early years may indeed involve Christian training—instruction in the Bible, teaching the child to pray, involvement in the church, and so forth—but it is not seen as the nurture of a *Christian* child. Initial nurture travels along tracks that will, the parents hope, eventually lead to conversion, but it is nurture of a pagan or unbelieving or neutral child. The child's Christian life begins only at a later stage, and it begins with an experience that is, to some extent at least, external to the normal processes of growth and maturation. This experience may occur in a church or Sunday School setting, but the Spirit initiates the Christian life from outside the normal tracks of nurture, and the rite of baptism is a sign that the child has responded in faith to the Spirit's call. From that point, the nurture of the new Christian child will take place along the tracks of instruction and involvement in the church, but these tracks are supplementary and additional to the tracks of original nurture.

---

and bread made in place of their ingredients, computers and spaceships formed from natural resources, formal gardens carved from the tangle of nature, and, I would add, creative human action forms new men. I develop this last point in relation to the ordination of priests in my doctoral dissertation, *The Priesthood of the Plebs: The Baptismal Transformation of Antique Order* (Cambridge), chap. 5. On *poesis* more generally, see John Milbank, *Theology and Social Theory: Beyond Secular Reason* (Oxford: Blackwell, 1990), 149–153, 218, 242; *The Word Made Strange: Theology, Language, Culture* (Oxford: Blackwell, 1997), 32, 73, 79, 123–144; *The Religious Dimension in the Thought of Giambattista Vico, 1668–1744: Volume I, The Early Metaphysics* (Lewiston: Edwin Mellen Press, 1991), passim. James B. Jordan makes a similar point in speaking about man as the "agent of transformation"; *Through New Eyes: Developing a Biblical View of the World* (Brentwood: Wolgemuth & Hyatt, 1988), chap. 10.

Infant baptism, by contrast, implies that instilling of Christ-like character runs along the tracks established in creation, for the Christian training of the child, of a *Christian* child, begins immediately upon his birth. God does not form a Christlike character by laying a second set of tracks but by restoring and transforming the "natural" tracks. From the beginning, consistent paedobaptists treat their children as Christians so that the social and cultural nurture of the child is simultaneously his or her nurture in Christian character and faith. This simultaneity recovers the condition of the original creation. If Adam had never sinned, he would have raised his children through instruction and certain forms of discipline (schedules, gradual introduction of responsibility, etc.),[17] and the result of this nurture would have been mature, godly character. The created means of nurture would have been simultaneously nurture and admonition in the Lord, so that coming to physical and psycho-social maturity would have been indistinguishable from coming to "religious" maturity. Sin is responsible for the gap that now exists. Because of the sins of parents and the original and actual sins of their children, it is possible for an infant to come to physical and a kind of psycho-social maturity without also growing in godliness. Paedobaptism implies that the gospel's solution to this gap is not to lay an entirely new set of tracks but to close the gap by redeeming the original created means from sin.

Infant baptism is thus consistent with the more general Reformed insistence that redemption is a renovation of creation spoiled by Adam rather than a new creation *ex nihilo*. Thus, Reformed theology implies that Christian character and Christian maturity are not instilled through means that are wholly separate from the way character is normally instilled. There is indeed a miracle involved, but it is a miracle brought to pass through created means, the miracle of

---

17. It seems likely that corporal discipline of a certain sort would have occurred even in a sinless world. Abel would, even if Adam had not sinned, been fascinated by fires and tried to reach into them. This is not in itself a sinful action, yet it would be, even in a sinless world, a dangerous action. Adam and Eve would have pulled him away from the fire to prevent him burning his hand, and that is at least a modest form of corporal coercion.

the daily sunrise that is so regular as to seem "natural" rather than the miracle of the lightning bolt from heaven.[18]

That is my general contention: that there are analogies between Christian nurture and "inculturation" or "socialization" into a particular way of life. Or, more neatly, Christian nurture is initiation and inculturation into the Christian culture that is the church. Here I am assuming the model of the church as Christian culture that I sketch in the article "Against Christianity: For the Church" elsewhere in this issue of *Biblical Horizons*. If the church is indeed a culture, then instilling Christian character is analogous to instilling character in other cultures. Groups display common characteristics not so much because of genetics and racial characteristics, though these factors should not be wholly discounted; primarily, individuals display the character common to their group because they have been nurtured in common habits, outlooks, aspirations, hopes. They have learned a common language, see their own lives and history in general in terms of a common story, and have a common outlook on life.[19]

---

18. Reformed theology also insists, of course, that God is free to work "outside" of His ordinary means, which means that He can bring someone to Himself through a lightning-bolt experience rather than through Christian nurture. It should be noted, however, first of all, that even a lightning bolt is a created means, and, secondly, that such experiences do not register apart from some kind of "ordinary" nurture. Jesus confronted Paul on the Damascus Road, but Paul had been trained from childhood in Pharisaical Judaism; Luther reputedly dedicated himself to the Lord's service following a harrowing thunderstorm, but Luther was already a child of the church. Apart from some kind of "ordinary nurture" in the faith, a lightning bolt is just a bolt from the blue; if it is to be perceived as a "message from God," some context of instruction must be presumed.

19. This might appear to be an "immanentization" of conversion and redemption, a reduction of salvation to sociology. In a creationist perspective, however, such a reduction is simply impossible. Every "social" factor that shapes our character depends entirely for its existence and its particular influence on the creative and providential action of God. Thus, social factors are never merely social; they are always secondary means, "instruments" wholly controlled by the hand of God. Nor is inculturation into a pagan way of life merely social; for the pagan is not neutral but a partaker in demons.

My point holds even if we consider an adult conversion and his subsequent baptism. Again, sin is the sole reason why anyone comes to maturity without being a worshiper of the Lord. In redeeming the adult unbeliever, however, the Spirit does not bypass the created means by which mature character is formed. The unbeliever will be confronted with the gospel through the witness of a believer—that is, through human language, conversation, debate, or through the believer's charitable action—or through contact with Scripture—which is created ink and paper. At his baptism, the adult convert becomes an "infant" in the church[20] and has to be re-nurtured through all the means of inculturation: teaching, discipline, rites of worship. Here, the Spirit's work is not so much to establish a brand new set of tracks as it is placing one who has been derailed back on the proper tracks.

In the following pages I want to fill in some details of this picture by considering what view of inculturation or discipleship emerges from infant baptism. Christian nurture runs along the (redeemed) tracks laid down in creation, but what are these tracks? I shall be guided by a reflection on certain features of a "phenomenological" analysis of infant baptism, and I shall be attempting to show, as I noted at the outset, that infant baptism is not "odd" but fits neatly with what we know about how the world really works. Keeping our sights focused on what is apparent in infant baptism, we can describe it as an external application of water that inducts the infant, through a symbolic action, into a community that he has not chosen. From this description, we can isolate the following features of paedobaptist nurture: the Spirit works 1) from outside in, 2) through unchosen circumstances and loyalties, 3) through communities, and 4) through symbols. Let us look at each of these elements in turn.

I

First, baptism is an *external* application of water, a striking fact that receives too little attention in theological literature on bap-

---

20. As is clearly implied in Matthew 18:1–6 and 1 John 2:12–14, for instance. Biblically speaking, all baptism is infant baptism.

tism. Much of the water symbolism in the Bible has to do with drinking: people thirst for God, God is the water that everlastingly satisfies all thirst, water in the wilderness is for the thirsty. These water themes do have some links with baptism,[21] but it still seems strange that baptism is applied to the outer body. Is it not the inner man that needs cleansing? And, is not the cleansing of the inner man precisely what the New Testament promises? Why not, then, a drinking rite, with the water of cleansing applied where it is needed? An external application of water fits better, it seems, in the Old Testament system, with its cleansing rites that removed "external" ceremonial defilement.[22]

Rather than change the rite that Jesus instituted, of course, we should take the oddness (to us) of its form as a starting point for reflection. If baptism is one of the means by which we are made disciples (Mt. 28:19–20), and if baptism marks us on the outside of the body, then it follows that we are made disciples from outside in.

Without wishing to claim that an "inside-out" pattern is unbiblical, in several senses the "outside-in" is the more basic movement. First, the Bible teaches that the Lord is the Savior, that man does not save himself, and therefore, his renewal must come from Someone else. We cannot rely on our own resources to make us become the kind of human beings we are created to be. Even if we concentrate on the work of the Spirit to renew the inner man, we must

---

21. One of the original elements of water symbolism in the Bible is the watering of the Garden of Eden (Gen. 2:5–6). Without water and a human caretaker, the land remains empty and unfruitful. Since humans are made of soil, watering of the soil to produce fruit is analogous to the Spirit's "watering" of dead flesh to produce fruitful human life. Compare 1 Corinthians 12:13, where the phrase translated as "drinking the Spirit" can be understood as "being watered" with the Spirit; Rudolf Schnackenberg, *Baptism in the Thought of St. Paul*, trans. G. R. Beasley-Murray (Oxford: Blackwell, 1964), 85.

22. The form of baptism thus challenges the belief that inner piety is the sole or primary location of religion; for the Bible "true religion" involves bringing the whole of life into conformity to the covenant. And, the church's continued use of a washing rite challenges the implicit Marcionism of much traditional and modern sacramental theology, for the sense that an external washing is out of place in the New Testament is a lingering trace of the notion that Old and New Covenants relate according to this ratio: Old:New::Material:Spiritual.

keep in mind that the Spirit comes from "outside," since He is God and we are not.[23] Our discipleship starts from the outside also in the sense that God chooses us and identifies us as His disciples and children before we respond; before we seek, we have already been found. This is to say that our identity as children of God is a gift coming from God, and not constructed from scratch.

Moreover, the means the Spirit uses to bring us to fellowship with Christ come from the outside. The gospel comes as an external word (*verbum ex auditu*). Whether we hear God speaking directly to us, or read the Scriptures, or listen to a sermon, the Word is communicated by another and confronts us from outside. We receive the Spirit by hearing, Paul says (Gal. 3:2), and we cannot believe without a preacher (Rom. 10:14). Belief unto salvation comes through the external means of the Word, which Peter, like Jesus, compares to a seed planted in the ground of our humanity (Mt. 13:19–23; 1 Pet. 1:23). The Word always comes to us in physical and therefore external form—marks on paper or vibrations in the air.

In its "outside-in" pattern, Christian discipleship follows the tracks laid down by creation. We can see this if we consider the place of moral prohibitions and sanctions in culture generally. Every culture, as Philip Rieff puts it, teaches its own rules of life, its own do's and don'ts, its "thou shalt nots," and every culture has a particular way of enforcing those "thou shalt nots." Cultural life involves, among other things, setting boundaries to human behavior and enforcing those boundaries. The boundaries taught and enforced by a culture do not, however, stay on the "outside" but

---

23. With respect to our relation with God, "inside" and "outside" become very difficult to distinguish if we operate within a fully creationist perspective. Since our existence is never autonomous, but at every moment and in every respect is dependent upon the action of the Spirit who is the Lord and Giver of life, then the Spirit is never "outside" in the way that other humans and things are outside. But this supports my point, namely, that our transformation into the image of Christ does not arise from resources that we possess in some independent fashion, since we possess no resources whatsoever in anything like an independent fashion. "Without Me you can do nothing" is an ontological as well as a soteriological claim.

become coordinates of one's map of reality and impress themselves on one's experience. As the Proverbs say, the rod and rebuke purge foolishness from the heart of a child (22:15; 23:13–14). Even when one resists external constraints, they have their internal effect; as Paul says, he would not have said "I will" in his heart if he had not first heard "thou shalt not" (Rom. 7:7–11). A milder example: How many adults raised in teetotaling households still feel a twinge of guilt when they sip their white wine?

In cultural life generally, external discipline and teaching form intellectual, moral, and practical habits, shaping personal character and identity. Infant baptism suggests that Christian nurture does not reject the "external" of cultural training in favor of purely internal transformation. Christ instead redeems the external.

Second, infant baptism imposes a religious identity that the infant *has not chosen*. As Rowan Williams puts it, it pushes choice to the side. Far from being a weakness, this is one of the strengths of infant baptism for Reformed theology, since it shows that God's approach to us precedes any response we make. The Divine Gardener loves us, waters us, cares for us, tends us before we can produce a thank offering in return. Infant baptism thus highlights the prevenience of grace.

The fact that infant baptism is unchosen forms the burden of Barth's early opposition to the practice, as he complains about the "violence" of imposing a religion on the infant without his or her consent. From Barth's perspective, infant baptism is a "wound" in the church; it is "arbitrary and despotic" to baptize infants, since confession and a request for baptism cannot be omitted without making baptism "an act of violence."[24] A moment's reflection reveals

---

24. Karl Barth, *The Teaching of the Church Regarding Baptism*, trans. Ernest A. Payner (London: SCM, 1948). Barth's more mature, less rhetorically harsh, considerations are found in *Church Dogmatics IV/4: The Christian Life (Fragment): Baptism as the Foundation of the Christian Life*, trans. G.W. Bromiley (Edinburgh: T&T Clark, 1969). Part of my goal in this paper is to meet Barth's challenge in this latter book that paedobaptists provide "evidence of [infant baptism's] inner necessity and therefore its theological credibility by the fact that one cannot speak of baptism at all without taking infant baptism into account." The doctrine of baptism would then become itself "implicitly and explicitly,

the palpable naivete of this objection. Everyone is born to some-one, into some social setting, and there are always not only social "givens" but religious ones as well. All parents have some religious leanings, even if they are only the leanings of indifference; the lib-eral parents who leave their child to decide his own religion are in-culcating a religion of toleration and pluralism and a corresponding intolerance of exclusive religions like Christianity. Infants are never brought up in a religiously neutral setting, having *no* religious iden-tity or biases imposed on them. If imposing religion on an infant is violence, *every* child is a victim of violence.[25]

Unchosen limits are, providentially, built into everyone's ini-tial situation. Every infant is born to a particular set of parents who have specific strengths and weaknesses, a particular configu-ration of genes, and unique interests and biases (including religious biases). These will affect the potential and nurture of their chil-dren. We are not fated to follow initial pathways—Michael Jackson could even change his skin—but our freedom to move into other pathways does not mean that none are originally marked out. The very fact that our choice of a different path is a choice of a *differ-ent* path shows that the original trajectory continues to play a cru-cial role in the narrative that defines who we are. Michael Jackson couldn't escape his starting point; if he bleached his skin, he was a black man who bleached his skin, but he could never be, simply, a "white man." If an Einstein arises from parents indifferent to sci-ence or education, he will be known as a "brilliant scientist who overcame tremendous obstacles." Personal identity and character

---

inclusively if not exclusively, the doctrine of infant baptism" rather than treat-ing infant baptism as a "supplement or appendix" (p. 169). This entire section, pages 169–178, should be carefully considered by anyone embarking on a the-ology of baptism.

25. Moreover, Barth's objection rests on the wholly unargued assumption that religious identity is secondary to "natural" identity, and does not enter into the basic symbolisms and disciplines that form a person. For Barth would have to admit that the individual who freely chooses to respond to God's call has already formed an identity of some sort. But this distinction of "natural" and "religious" identity is precisely the question at issue between Baptists and pae-dobaptists, as I indicated above.

are *always* and permanently shaped by the relations, loyalties, and circumstances into which we are thrown.

The coming of a new creation does not dissolve the web of unchosen circumstances into a shapeless mound to be molded by autonomous choice and consent.[26] What is good or evil is the way of life itself, not whether it is "freely" chosen.[27] Contrary to existentialists, the human problem is not that we face unchosen givens; the tragedy of the human situation does not lie in our "thrownness." Adam was thrown into a garden, wholly without his consent, and yet the Lord said that Adam's situation was "very good." The problem then is not the reality of unchosen constraints and givens but the nature of those givens; the tragedy of the human situation— which is not really tragedy in the classical sense—is that the trajectory of human life in Adam is a trajectory toward the grave.[28]

From the perspective of infant baptism, we can see that what the gospel announces is not absolute choice, but an alternative givenness, equally unchosen. Baptism does not liberate us from society, but from *Adamic* society, with all its pathologies. Baptism engrafts us into an alternative society that, like the old society, begins to impose its patterns on an infant as soon as he enters it. Life still begins with a trajectory, but this alternative givenness has been reordered and redeemed so that its trajectory is directed (however

---

26. One of the great challenges to Baptist theology, one that has not, to my knowledge, been accepted, is to justify theologically the transition from the Old order, where choice was obviously not the be-all and end-all of the religion of Yahweh, to the New order, where choice, on the Baptist view, takes a much more prominent, even crucial, role. What is it about the life, death, and resurrection of Jesus that justifies this fundamental difference in the shape of religious life?

27. The notion that one can choose in a wholly unconstrained way partakes of the Enlightenment illusion of autonomy. Choices are inevitably constrained by our understanding of a given situation (always severely limited by innumerable factors), by pressures from family, friends, and even strangers, by our resources of imagination and courage. "Free choice," by contrast, assumes an autonomous chooser who takes his stance—impossibly—"above" all these constraining factors, a chooser who occupies either no place in particular or the place of God.

28. As Van Til never tires of saying, the human problem is ethical, not ontological: due to sin, not inherent in being a creature.

imperfectly) toward righteousness and life. The order of redemption is following the tracks of the order of creation: In both cases we are thrown into situations that are not of our own choosing, and in both cases our religious identity is initially not a matter of our consent and choice. As we are to grow to appreciate the wisdom of our parents, so we are eventually to embrace and love what came to us before our arms could reach for it.

We have already anticipated the third point: If we are formed from outside, confronted with unchosen influences from the moment we are born, it is because we are born into *communities*, into relationships. Primarily, I mean our relationship with God. The fact I exist at all is a gift, which means my existence is preceded by the act of a Giver; anything I do is necessarily secondary, always a response to His initial donation. I do not come to be who I am and *then* enter a relation with God; I come to be who I am through the relation I already have with God (whether one of friendship or enmity). My first move is never absolutely first, but always a countermove to God's initiative and to the initiative of those whom He providentially places in my way.

Rosenstock-Huessy's grammatical sociology is helpful in explaining this point. In real social life, Rosenstock-Huessy points out, "I" is not the first person. Long before we can say "I," and before we have any consciousness of being an "I," we are being addressed by others. "Thou," not "I" is the real first person. Descartes said *"Cogito ergo sum"* ("I think, therefore I am") but long before he could say *cogito*, someone had said to him, *cogita*; and before he could say *sum* someone had said *es*. Thus, Rosenstock-Huessy substituted for the Cartesian *Cogito* the motto: "I respond, though I shall be changed" (*Respondeo, etsi mutabor*), which implies, among many other things, that I do not stand alone but am from the beginning confronted with others.[29] Infant baptism suggests that the place of the community in

---

29. See Eugen Rosenstock-Huessy, *Out of Revolution: Autobiography of Western Man* (Providence: Berg [1938] 1993), chap. 18; *Speech and Reality* (Norwich: Argo Books, 1970), passim, esp. 86; *I Am an Impure Thinker* (Norwich: Argo Books, 1970), passim, esp. chaps. 1 and 5.

shaping the individual is not canceled by the gospel; in the church our *credo* is simply a variation of *respondeo*.

Self-image is likewise formed in relation to others. I do not wish to swallow up the individual's contribution here, or to deny individual responsibility, but simply to suggest that the individual's contribution to his self-image is, in practice, impossible to pry apart from the contribution of others. Christian counselor Leanne Payne tells of many she has counseled whose self-image was perverted by their parents' attitudes and actions toward them. In one case, a man told of how his mother put him in dresses because she had wanted a girl, and Payne describes how this inhibited the man's ability to be comfortable with his masculinity. He had been treated and judged as a girl and this had molded his self-image.[30]

Healing for such a person does not come by the bootstrap method; a new, more accurate, more healthy self-image will, like his perverse self-image, be offered by others. Thus, here also, redemption follows the tracks laid out in creation.[31] Ultimately, our identity is defined by how God judges us, and our self-image is to conform to His judgment. Accordingly, Paul constantly tells his readers to "consider yourselves" as dead to sin, as justified, forgiven sinners; Christians are to have a self-image not based on our own perceptions or feelings but based on the Word and promise of God. Our self-image is to be reformed by Someone Else's image of us.

But how do we come to know God's judgment of us? God has not appeared to announce His verdict of justification to me, nor have I heard His voice. Rather, His verdict is announced through other people, through the church, so my self-image is formed by the verdict of God as mediated by the verdict of the church. Each one who receives the Spirit becomes a spring or fountain overflowing

---

30. See Leanne Payne, *The Broken Image* (Grand Rapids: Baker, 1981); *Crisis in Masculinity* (Grand Rapids: Baker, 1985); *The Healing of the Homosexual* (Downers Grove: Crossway, 1985).

31. Note I am not saying that Christian self-image is attached to a more basic self-image; rather, Christian self-image is formed in the same way that perverse, Adamic self-image is formed: that is, in important part by the judgments of others.

with the Spirit to others (Jn. 7:37–38), and one gift of the water of the Spirit is authority to cleanse, to forgive and remit sins (Jn. 20:22–23).[32] Parents who constantly remind us that we belong to Christ, ministers who week by week pronounce absolution, fellow believers who communicate the love of God in word and deed—these are the means by which God's gracious Word comes to us and forms our identity as believers.

Fourth and finally, the "inculturation" of the infant into the Christian culture of the church takes place through *symbols*. Confusion concerning symbols and symbolism is so pervasive among Christians, especially evangelical Protestants, that a few comments on the role of symbolism need to be made. First, symbols do not merely express what we already know and desire but also shape knowledge and desire. The clearest example of this is language, a system of symbolic sounds and visual shapes that forms our thoughts and guides our basic perceptions of reality. When we look around us, we do not, as empiricism suggests, receive sense impressions in the raw but experience the world under a certain description. When we look at a chair, we do not merely receive visual sense impressions; we see the chair as a chair, under the description provided by the linguistic symbol. Acts of perception and observation include a moment of interpretation, and interpretation inevitably involves language. Thus, for example, one's experience of an unexpected death in the family will be influenced by the description he puts on it: Is it a "meaningless tragedy" or part of the "discipline of a loving Father"? One of the effects of saturation in Scripture is that we gain the linguistic and mental equipment to grasp the world as it truly is and to live in it fruitfully.

Even what we think of as most deeply our own, as our deepest personal feelings, desires and aspirations, are formed by the symbols

---

32. Compare the frequency of exhortations to "forgive one another" in the New as opposed to the Old Testament. The Pharisees may have been unbalanced, but one can understand how they might conclude from the Old Testament that "no one can forgive sins but God alone." Yet, the New Testament consistently exhorts the Spirit-filled people of God to carry out the divine office of forgiveness.

of the communities in which we are nurtured. Children aspire to be film or sports stars, and these aspirations touch their identity to such an extent that they become defined by their aspirations. But where do these desires come from? Surely they are not generated from "inside." Would anyone spend his youth striving to "be like Mike" if "Mike" had not become an icon of physical grace and material success? The desires and aspirations of these children are formed by the symbols that are available in the society. A young man in Papua New Guinea may aspire to be like the Head Man, but that he should aspire to "be like Mike" will never enter his head.[33] Identity, with its aspirations and desires, is shaped by those whom we choose to imitate, those who serve as "types" into whose image we wish to be molded. Paul recognizes this human capacity for imitation of a symbolic person and frequently tells his readers to follow his example as he has followed Jesus (1 Cor. 4:16; 11:1; Phil. 3:17; 4:9; 1 Thes. 1:6; 2 Thes. 3:9). The Bible gives us many "symbols" in this sense, many "types" that are to impress themselves on us.

Second, symbols are not merely "pointers" to the real world but are tools by which we operate the real world. "Stop that!" said by a parent to a child does not describe the world but seeks to change it.

I do not want to trivialize the question, but from the perspective I have been outlining, we might say that the question, "Why baptize infants?" is similar to the question, "Why speak to infants?" Why talk to them when they cannot understand anything you say? The answer is of course that it is through speaking to them that they learn to understand and even to speak for themselves. Unless we deploy linguistic symbols in their direction, they will not develop the skills they need. Similarly, we do not baptize babies because they understand what is happening to them, but in order that they might come to that understanding. Through the water of baptism, God speaks to infants so they might come to know and love Him. And through that symbol and others, they are trained to respond.

---

33. René Girard has, in a number of works, argued that our desires are largely "mimetic," imitative of the desires and aspirations of others.

To make some final comments about baptism, let me bring together the communal dimension of nurture and what we are saying about symbols, for it is involvement in community that gives
effect to symbols and rites. In anthropological literature, one of the
prominent classes of ritual consists of "rites of passage" that conduct a person across a social and cultural boundary, from one status
to another. A wedding rite moves a woman from "bachelorette" to
"wife"; ordination from "member" to "pastor."

Pierre Bourdieu has argued that the status conferred in a rite
must be constantly reaffirmed by the community for the "magic" of
ritual to have its effect.[34] William Jefferson Clinton is inaugurated
President, and what makes this rite of passage real is that there-
after everyone treats Mr. Clinton differently. Everyone defers to
him, calls him by his new name—"Mr. President"—cozies up to
him seeking support for legislation or urging him to ignore human
rights abuses in Indonesia or China. Each of these is a reaffirma-
tion of his new status, and each affirmation reminds Bill Clinton
of his status and the obligations it places on him. He is constantly
challenged to make what the Westminster Larger Catechism might
have called an "improvement" on his inauguration, to live up to the
obligations imposed by the rite of inauguration.

We can see how this applies to baptism. James Jordan has re-
peatedly said that we should count and treat the baptized as Christians. That is correct, but it would be a mistake to understand this
as something purely "external" and "outside"—that has nothing to
do with who we really are, as a game of "let's pretend." Counting
and treating the baptized as Christians is one of the important
ways in which their Christian identity becomes internalized and
the Christian culture of the church becomes formative of their personal character. Of course, it can lead to presumption; those who
are judged believers by others can come to believe that they are in-
vulnerable to apostasy, that no matter how they live and behave,
they are secure in their relationship with God. While there is no

---

34. Pierre Bourdieu, *Language and Symbolic Logic*, ed. John B. Thompson,
trans. Gino Raymond and Matthew Adamson (Cambridge: Polity Press,
1991), chap. 4.

guaranteed way to prevent presumption, it should be said that one who lives in rebellion against God should no longer be judged as a believer by other believers. The point here is that, like the people who call Bill Clinton "Mr. President," parents and others who treat a baptized infant as a Christian are reaffirming his status, improving the rite of baptism, making it effective. The status of "member of Christ" that was conferred in baptism thereby becomes internalized as the baptized person, treated as a believer, comes to see himself as others see him, and comes to accept the obligations that the rite has imposed on him.

Too often, Reformed paedobaptists have not "counted and treated" baptized children as Christians. This not only undermines the theological credibility of the paedobaptist position, but has the serious practical effect of making the baptized uncertain of his status in the church and in Christ. To baptize a child and then to say that he or she cannot really be a member of the covenant people until he does X or Y, until he has a certain kind of experience or a certain level of knowledge that he can articulate to the satisfaction of church authorities, is to undermine everything baptism communicated. It is as if after his inauguration everyone insisted on calling Bill Clinton "Bubba" and treating him with contempt. If we baptize infants and treat them as pagans, they receive at best a conflicting message, and uncertainty about their standing in Christ is sure to result. The efficacy of infant baptism is bound up with "counting and treating," with the continuing reinforcement of this status by other members of the church, who, filled with the Spirit, are also mediators of the Spirit.

I'm especially talking about paedocommunion. Washing in Scripture and in cultural life generally is frequently in preparation for a meal, a dimension of baptismal imagery that is supported by the "clothing" imagery of Galatians 3:27. Bathing our children and dressing them in Christ, but then refusing to let them sit at the table in the kingdom, is profoundly incoherent both as theology and practice. If we wish to see baptism work its "magic," this is the place to begin.

II

This discussion will, I hope, have helped to indicate the depth o the differences between Baptist and paedobaptist practice and the ology, which are perhaps revealed most clearly when the sociolog ical implications (which are also soteriological) are teased out.[35] For the paedobaptist, the gospel announces and brings into par tial (pre-eschatological) realization the renovation of the creation and of human life. For the paedobaptist, Jesus is the Last Adam, who, by undoing the work of the first Adam, enables His people to pursue the program of dominion that Adam failed to fulfill. Jesus opens heaven to His people and promises eternal fellowship in His kingdom, to be sure, but His mission was equally to ensure that the Father's will is done on earth as it is in heaven.

Baptists may sometimes say the same, but their practice moves them in a different direction. For Baptist practice, redemption— inclusion in the new humanity that is the church—adds a second layer of "religious" life to the "natural" life of creation. This is nec essarily the case, since children begin their "natural" life of physical and socio-cultural growth before coming to faith. This dualism of nature/culture and religion means that Christ is not in a full sense "New Adam" who inaugurates a race that will fulfill Adam's call ing to dominion. Frequently, the tracks laid down by Christ are believed to lead to a different destination than that envisioned in the original creation. God commanded Adam to have dominion on earth, whereas Christ provides a "spiritual" and purely heavenly re demption. Instead of equipping them for godly dominion on earth, Christian faith and nurture in the church prepares believers more or less exclusively for eternal life in heaven.

The sociology implied by each understanding of redemption diverges significantly. As a sign of the gospel, the baptism of infants indicates that even from their earliest years God intends His chil dren to live Christian lives in the Spirit, and to be embraced by the Christian culture of the church. The Baptist position implies the

---

35. I was helped toward this formulation by comments made by James Jordan at the Biblical Horizons Summer Conference, June 1996, where this portion of the chapter was presented as a lecture.

opposite, since for Baptists the Christian culture of the church does not formally claim children in their infancy or in their earliest nurture. Even when Baptists are willing to treat their children in some sense as "Christian" children, their baptismal practice implies that the early years of their children's lives are not years of "Christian" living. Christian character is thus something "added" to the character that they begin to develop in their earliest years. Thus Christian faith, language, and culture is a religious addition to culture, language, and everyday life. For children will certainly develop *some* kind of character. Baptist children learn language from infancy, but they will not learn Christian language as *their* language; they will participate in rites, but not Christian rites; they will be subject to discipline, but not (explicitly) Christian discipline. In short, they will be inculturated into *some* culture but that culture is not going to be explicitly or consistently Christian. Neither, however, is that culture going to be religiously neutral, since such neutrality is impossible. In the absence of formal and official inculturation into the church's form of life, Baptist parents, if they consistently maintain their position, are left to take their cues more or less from the surrounding culture. Thus, Baptist nurture has an inherent tendency toward worldliness, toward accommodation with the surrounding culture.[36]

Let me press this polemic a step or two further. By maintaining the gap between "natural" life and nurture and Christian life and nurture, Baptist theology and practice perpetuates and exaggerates cultural currents that produced the secular world beginning in the late medieval period. By positing a distinction between natural life and natural teleology over and against supernatural life and supernatural teleology, and by suggesting that natural life (which includes cultural and political life) had its own integrity that needs

---

36. I must insist, of course, that what I am attacking are not individual Baptist parents but the logic and outcome of their position. Many Baptists are far better in practice than their theology warrants; they nurture their children as Christians, teaching them Christian language and applying Christian discipline, and thus tend to be functional paedobaptists. But the ambiguity of the child's status in the Baptist view casts a shadow of ambiguity over the whole process.

only to be "completed" by the supernatural addition of grace, scholastic theology wrote the preamble to nature and culture's "declaration of independence" from God. In modern culture, this gap has widened, and the supernatural realm is gradually forced out of view altogether, often by being confined to the spirituality of the inner heart.

Baptist theology does not operate with an explicit nature/supernature distinction, but many of its responses to infant baptism accept the modern view of religion as a matter of the heart. For Paul K. Jewett, the Old Covenant was external, national, and material, while the New is internal, individual, and spiritual.[37] Such a position concedes that the entire public world of politics, economics, international relations, and so forth, is outside specifically religious concern. One might find ways within such a theology to bring Christian principles to bear on these spheres, to bridge the gap between "religion" and most of the remainder of life. Certainly Christians operating on something like Jewett's view are engaged in these various areas of life, no doubt working out their faith as well as they can and pleasing the Lord in the process. Such efforts are, however, in spite of their fundamental theology rather than because of it. For the New Testament, the gospel is about the renewal of creation by the work of Christ so that absolutely nothing is outside its scope. It is, as Leslie Newbigin insists, "public truth," an announcement of a set of historical events with public, observable historical consequences. Because it does not insist on this gospel, Baptist theology and practice is complicit with modern secularism's confinement of the church to "spiritual" matters and of religion to the "heart."

Baptists will doubtless respond to these assertions with profound astonishment. Normally precisely the opposite argument is

---

37. Paul K. Jewett, *Infant Baptism and the Covenant of Grace* (Grand Rapids: Eerdmans, 1978), 90–91; see also Barth, *Church Dogmatics* IV/4, 178, who states that the "people of the new covenant is not a nation" but a "people freely and newly called and assembled out of Israel and all nations." For a strong affirmation of the contrary, see George Lindbeck, "The Gospel's Uniqueness: Election and Untranslatability," *Modern Theology* 13 (1997), esp. 446–447.

made, and passionately: Paedobaptists sanctify culture and thus tend toward accommodation with the world. Barth, for example, charges that infant baptism remains the practice of Western churches only because the churches do not want to give up the notion that society and church are coextensive, because they cling to a dream of Christendom whose reality has evaporated.[38] There is some historical truth to this claim, for in both West and East, to varying degrees in different times and places, the churches have become entangled with the existing culture to the extent that baptism became a cultural "initiation" rather than a rebirth into Christ's new culture. To this day in England, citizens have the right to have their children christened by the Church of England, though they have no other interest in or connection to the church. This is abominable, but it is not inherent in the paedobaptist position.

Correctly understood and practiced, infant baptism is induction into a *separate* culture, a *separated* and holy people, not induction into the larger world culture. Regarding "separateness," paedobaptists and Baptists agree. The issue that divides is whether or not what is "separate" is in fact a *culture*, rather than a religious organization. For if it is a culture, then the church has its own internal political and social configuration, its own language, rites, and disciplines, and has the goal of conveying its way of life to the next generation.

The question can be phrased as follows: How wide is the embrace of this separate culture? Is it a separate way of life or is it a separate way of *religious* life in the narrowed modern sense? Does this culture include people in every stage of life, or does it only include those who have reached a certain level of maturity? Is the church a new *humanity* that includes humans of all levels of intelligence, maturity, and giftedness, or is it more an organization for the religiously interested or the religiously mature? Does the church consist wholly of Christians (infants, children, youth, and adults), or is the community that assembles each Lord's day internally divided between Christians and their neutral or unbelieving children? Is

---

38. Barth, *The Teaching of the Church Regarding Baptism*, 52–54.

that assembly *entirely* a separate people, or does the world intrude into the church in the form of unbaptized children? Where is the line between the Christian culture of the church and the world—at the baptismal borders of the church or along a baptismal boundary that runs through the midst of the assembled people?[39] If the church is a culture, if it is the new humanity in Christ, then it includes all aspects of life and all sorts and conditions of men.

To this point, I have spoken of infant baptism on a theological level, but it is of course a practice as well as a doctrine. Infant baptism thus not only "implies" that the church is Christian culture and that the gospel announces the coming of a new creation into the midst of the old, but it also brings into being the church as Christian culture and is an instrument for the renovation of creation. Without claiming to be exhaustive, let me make a suggestion about how this works: Parents have their infants baptized. If they are self-conscious about the meaning of that baptism, they treat their children as believers, teaching them to speak "Bible" and to understand the world in biblical terms, leading them in their increasingly active participation in Christian rites, bringing them into submission to Christian discipline. The children are inculturated into Christian culture: They are not shaped (primarily) by the national culture in which they live and then, in addition at some second stage, into Christian culture; the formative culture *is* the Christian culture of the church. Thus, infant baptism, when its implications are properly understood and followed through, actually forms Christian culture as an intergenerational project by inculturating the next generation.

If infants are *not* baptized, and (consistently) not treated as Christians, if they are not taught Christian language and the Christian story as *their* language and story, if they do not participate in Christian rites, if they are not molded by Christian discipline—then we should expect that the church will not be the

---

39. In no way am I denying that there are "false sons" in the pale of the church. This does not, however, undermine the fact that baptism is the boundary of the church, any more than the presence of traitors in a nation dissolves national borders.

ntergenerational project of Christian culture and the world will not be renovated. For the refusal to baptize infants carries the implication that a whole sector of life—cultural nurture and all the institutional, social, and political supports that this involves—is outside the realm of specifically religious interest. If infants are not baptized, we would expect that the world would intrude instead into the church.

In America, where Baptistic theology has been dominant since the revivals of the eighteenth century, this is precisely what has happened. The church has been coopted by the American story and become an appendage to the American democratic experiment; the Fourth of July receives more attention in many American churches than Pentecost. The church's rites are not considered important by members or by the leadership; cultural rites of passage and cultural "feast days" take priority. Church discipline is sporadic and weak, and worldly values and behavior are as likely to be found among Christians as among unbelievers. Christians no longer have a sense of living in a world that is different from the world surrounding them, because they are *not* living in a different world. At best, Christians are internally divided, with one foot in and one without Christian culture, speaking Zion on Sunday and the language of Ashdod during the week. And they are divided or completely assimilated because infant baptism has not, along with the Word, Supper, and Discipline, formed Christian culture in the church.[40]

I began with the observation that Baptist theology and practice seems reasonable and natural and that infant baptism seems odd and weird. I hope that I have at least begun to provide a plausible argument that shows the logic of infant baptism and demonstrates its consistency with the way things really are. But the apparent rea-

---

40. Baptists are not, as I noted above, alone at fault for this. Far too many paedobaptists fail to work out the implications of infant baptism in their nurture and church practice. This failure is apparent not only in the European state churches, but also in the United States, where many paedobaptists fail to nurture their children as Christians. But the most glaring failure here is the widespread practice of refusing to give children access to the Lord's Table.

sonableness of the Baptist position still needs to be accounted for
I would suggest that Baptist theology and baptismal practice seem
reasonable and natural only because our definitions of "reasonable
and natural" are thoroughly infected with the modern notion that
consent is the alpha and omega of social, moral, and religious life
For moderns, only a freely, autonomously chosen action is morally
laudable, and submitting to an imposed religious obligation is con
demned as heteronomy. There is a vicious circle involved here, for in
America, Baptist theology and practice has promoted the primacy
of choice, and has thereby shaped a world in which Baptist theology
and practice seem transparently reasonable. If we break out of that
circle and dethrone consent, and the variety of implications that
cluster around it, the Baptist position loses a great deal of its force
What I have tried to do is to show that infant baptism is actually
more consistent with what we know of how the world works than
believer's baptism, though this point has been obscured by the illusion of modern prejudice.

Made in the USA
Las Vegas, NV
26 May 2024

90394324R00085